Getting a
Life

OLDER PEOPLE TALKING

Edited by

MICHAEL SIMMONS

ISIS

LARGE PRINT
Oxford

First published in Great Britain 2000
by Peter Owen Publishers

Published in Large Print 2002 by ISIS Publishing Ltd.
7 Centremead, Osney Mead, Oxford OX2 0ES
by arrangement with Peter Owen Publishers

British Library Cataloguing in Publication Data
Getting a life: older people talking – Large print ed.
1. Aged – Great Britain – Social conditions
2. Aged – Great Britain – Social life and customs
3. Old age – Great Britain 4. Large type books
I. Simmons, Michael, 1935 –
305.2′6

ISBN 0–7531–5627–X (hb)
ISBN 0–7531–5628–8 (pb)

Printed and bound by Antony Rowe, Chippenham

Contents

Introduction

When Help the Aged, as the originators of this book, invited me to edit it and prepare it for the publishers, I soon realized it would be a radical departure from anything I had done in my previous working life. This had largely consisted of nearly forty years of commissioning, editing and writing for what are sometimes called serious newspapers. But this exercise taught me very quickly a great deal about people, young as well as old, and how they handle each other. The exchanges which I had while the book was in progress revealed much to me about how different individuals see the passing of a lifetime and, most important of all, what it means to be an older person in Britain today. It very quickly became clear that there is a lot of justified anger and resentment, as well as undisguised joy and pleasure, about the environment in which so many of us find ourselves in our later years.

When we become "older people", at whatever age, we do not transform into a new species, but we do begin a new life. Like it or not, we have an unfamiliar role to play. After all, the parameters of every moment of our lives are suddenly different from what they were before; the rules governing our behaviour have been rewritten overnight, which means that all our aspirations, ambitions and expectations have to change accordingly. It also means that our relationships with people may have to change — sometimes imperceptibly but often fundamentally. We have sought in this little book to take account of these things.

Help the Aged and I agreed at a very early stage that we did not want this to be a handbook. There are plenty of those around already, and some of them are of high quality. Rather, we wanted to present on the printed page the thoughts and words of older people now, so that others might become more aware of their thinking. These essays are, if you like, contributions to a debate which is only now beginning to take off in a meaningful way. The new millennium has seen the start of what one national newspaper leader-writer has called "the start of pensioner pulling power". The debate is one which it would be a mistake to ignore.

The individuals who came forward to contribute are, like the essays which carry their names, very varied in character and in the nature of their personal convictions. Each of them was asked to produce a personal and preferably reflective 2,000-word essay on an agreed theme. It was to be based on their own experience over the years and it was to draw on the views and the attitudes they had formed in the light of that experience. Beyond that, there were no holds barred: they were told they could be as polemical and serious, or as light-hearted and frivolous, as they wished.

This means there are analytical thoughts alongside thoughts which are more anecdotal. Some of the pieces — and not necessarily those emanating from politicians! — are more political than others. Interestingly, there are also some that convey a coherent message simply through the glimpses they give which are purely autobiographical. I hope that this variety is reflected in the pages that follow.

During the collating and editing phase there were suggestions from some quarters that we had succumbed to bias and selectivity. "What about my mum" was the rhetorical challenge from a friend, now in his early fifties. "She lives alone, not far from the British Museum and five minutes by bus from the heart of the West End. But she's not well off, not at all, and she has personally never been in the West End. She goes for days without seeing another soul, and her life can be pretty bloody empty. How many people like her have you catered for"

It was a good question, a rebuke in its way which was as purposely disconcerting as it was unambiguous. But it is one which we would like to think has been dealt with implicitly, if not explicitly, between these covers. Life was by no means always comfortable for the individuals writing here, and it is not invariably comfortable now. Read these essays and along the way you really will become very aware of the predicament of people like my friend's mum. But read also, where you are able, between the more assertive lines and you will find there are not a few solutions being offered to the sort of problems that confront people like her.

Some of the contributors are household names, while others will be completely unknown outside the circles in which they move. No matter. Everyone has a contribution to make, and every contribution has its own validity. All of them have shown, forthrightly and often quite deliberately, that older people in general, at the start of the third millennium in Britain, are not lacking in resilience. All in all, there is no shortage of ideas on how to make ends meet, to make friends, to pass the time or even, in the language of the moment, to "get a life".

What all the contributors have in common (except one of them, who edges in through a side door because she has spent her career working closely with and for older people) is that they are all over sixty. A handful of them will not see ninety again. Some individuals whom I approached categorically refused to contribute, saying — a touch sniffily — that they didn't think of themselves in terms of being "old" and therefore they couldn't write anything helpful. That point of view is a matter for argument, but they couldn't be persuaded. A number of people, including some very distinguished people in the public eye, wished the project well, saying that they would love to have written but they were "so busy". One of these said he was currently deeply embroiled in a political debate about the future of Iraq, while another said he was very sorry but he had to get on with a new television series he was preparing about mammals and the way they live.

Everyone who has written has something to say. Their words provide irrefutable evidence that experience and the passing of the years have not inclined them to take things easy. Rather the opposite. One of the oldest of them regaled me at length and very forcefully in a long-distance telephone call with exhortations to be more angry. "What on earth has happened to outrage" she demanded. "There is a hell of lot in this life to be outraged about, and yet people are taking it all so easy. There are so many things to be downright furious about, and I'm not just talking about things affecting old people. We want more outrage!"

With such words ringing in my ears, it was inevitable that I was kept awake for much of the night that followed by notions of the sort of new old militants (in the good old-fashioned sense of the word) who might be at the barricades in the coming decades of this new century, fighting for the cause of older people and their rights. If these barricades turn out to have been designed and built in a corner of Liverpool by a still feisty one-time suffragette, I shall be rather pleased and not in the least surprised.

★ ★ ★

Coming to terms with the new life, the subject of the first section of this book, is a philosophical thing. We may not become all that different, but we do have to reflect on where we are at and where we may be going. Denis Healey brings a characteristic candour to bear, pithily and a touch poignantly, making it clear there are pluses as well as minuses. Peter Preston scrutinizes a new older life as a grandparent, while Jean Reid ponders whether or not the new life is, or isn't, a matter of "joining". Kurt Strauss manages quirkily to face both ways from a resolutely suburban viewpoint.

Taking stock is something that all older people do, every so often. Thus Claire Rayner assesses where she is at, having moved from a materially deprived childhood into a well-heeled later life, while Monty Meth considers what he has encountered and still encounters, through so-called "ageism", in the way of prejudice. Vera Ivers looks at the experience of her friends, while Paulette Bauckham discusses taking stock in the context of reminiscence. Ivor Smith-Cameron surveys how growing older is seen by different religious faiths, and Gillian Ford, whose hospice work has given her such unique qualifications, ponders ways of coming to terms with death.

Managing — *or coping* — requires cash and will-power as well as know-how and skill. It also requires, whenever possible, decent and viable pension arrangements, and who better to wrestle with such a question than the doughty Barbara

Castle? It also entails balancing budgets and possible belt-tightening, which are areas of perennial concern to Dave Goodman, and also making the most appropriate buying and selling decisions, here examined by Michael Dunne. Giving and taking love in its various forms is the theme of Angela Willans and, since no management of any sort is feasible without health, Gordon Macpherson offers a prognosis and prognosticates accordingly.

Getting a life requires effort. Angela Graham was at first confronted with a vacuum but then found herself on a new learning curve, while Margaret Simey triumphantly found her treasured independence where she least expected it. Eric Midwinter suggests that education, in a very broad sense, may provide answers, while Peter Laslett turns his qualified attention to universities and Barrie Porter argues that grappling with the internet need not be so very daunting.

Making the most of it is what happens once *getting a life* has been accomplished. Pushpa Chaudhary has been making the most of it since she came to Britain from India in the early 1960s, while Mary Stott, well into her nineties, assiduously nurses her hobbies and Tony Carter suggests keeping on speaking up. Elisabeth de Stroumillo continues, with or without a stick to aid her, to travel, while Mike Banks indefatigably goes on climbing. Jean Burton and her husband took the bit between their teeth early on and upped and went — starting again in every way.

On second thoughts, we don't have a different role to play when we become an older person. We have several — and we can play quite a number of them at the same time.

Happy reading!

Michael Simmons
London, September 2000

Acknowledgements

Tessa Harding, at Help the Aged, rang me out of the blue and asked me to produce this book. How I did it and whom I should invite to contribute were largely left to me, and I enjoyed the task enormously. Ann-Louise Hobcraft was Ann-Louise Limm when it started, and she too gave me a free hand, as did Sandra Chalmers. Alison Giordimaina and Emma Hodges have been very helpful throughout.

COMING TO TERMS

Denis Healey

Peter Preston

Jean Reid

Kurt Strauss

DENIS HEALEY

And louder sing . . .

Personally, I did not notice much change until I was seventy-five. From that age on I have found my memory deteriorating and my senses getting less acute. I can mistake a reference to "Stena Sealink" on television for "Denis Healey". I can distinguish between different vowels, but all consonant sounds are the same to me. I can fail to see something I am looking at when it is staring me in the face.

There is a saying that when you are old you either widen or wizen. I have done both. Physically I have wizened; I lost two stones in weight between the ages of seventy-five and seventy-seven. I can no longer run upstairs as I used to do. I find travel very tiring. Psychologically I have widened. I am much more interested in people as human beings and can imagine them at every age from childhood onwards when I see them.

I have lost all my interest in power and position and no longer worry about making money. I still enjoy my work, but only what I want to do —

talking to business audiences about financial matters and to meetings of the National Trust about my favourite countryside.

I am now much more sensitive to colours, shapes and sounds. My eye will automatically compose a clump of flowers or a corner of a landscape in a picture. I enjoy music even more than I used to because I get greater pleasure out of the sound of different instruments.

I have become exceptionally sensitive to sunlight, which immediately moves me to pleasure. I use my increased leisure to look at paintings wherever there is a gallery, to enjoy opera and drama at a theatre, to visit country houses.

I love my wife, my children and grandchildren more than ever and have much more time with them.

To use Freud's expression — I have lost interest in my ego, much preferring my superego, while my id continues to wane.

I have always felt that the best comment on old age was written by the poet W.B. Yeats, in his poem "Sailing to Byzantium":

An aged man is but a paltry thing
A tattered coat upon a stick, unless
Soul clap its hands and sing, and louder sing
For every tatter in its mortal dress . . .

PETER PRESTON

Divides don't work

The stereotype, when you think about it, is just as bad as the blonde bimbos of advertising. They jiggle their way to a sale while we put on our woolly cardigans, our best set of teeth, our soppiest smiles. We are the Werther Originals, as depicted in the commercials of ITV. We are your typical granddad. The dregs of the summer wine before winter comes. Have a sticky toffee, Papa, and hope it doesn't lose you another filling.

Yet the reality, of course, is quite different. Always will be and, in my memory, always was. My own granddad would never have dreamed of handing round the sweet packets. They were works of the Devil. Nor, if truth be told, was he much into cardigans or bed-time cuddles. He was a retired primary school headmaster, trained in the austere days before the First World War. He was available for visits on alternate Sundays (when the routine did not vary). Morning service at the grey granite chapel in the village. A small roast with boiled potatoes and watery greens.

15

Sunday school in the hall behind the chapel. Tea — and off you go home.

The compensations (in no particular order, with no particular attractions) were: (a) the right to eat windfall apples providing they were too bruised or mouldy to fill a pie; (b) the opportunity to play games in the bomb shelter built into the heart of the rockery, with its darkness and satisfyingly slimy walls; (c) the possibility — if left alone — of stroking the stuffed frog in the front parlour.

The visits ceased two years after my father's (young and sudden) death when my mother married his oldest, kindest friend and we found ourselves no longer welcome in the granite chapel or the kitchen of watery greens, having somehow broken one of Granddad's rules of protracted mourning. The severance, in context, was not much mourned itself. It never occurred to me that grandfathers could be figures of affection or utility. They were, in an era not yet quite passed from memory, dour and forbidding figures. My wife's grandfather, returning from work, would have high tea brought to him on a tray while his children sat silently in the next room. They were the nuisance; he was the fountainhead.

And now? Now, joyously, all is utterly changed. The family isn't a succession of closed doors and patriarchal rigidities. It is being part of a team. It is the sudden return, late in life, of a once-remembered usefulness. The world is not merely changed but transformed.

The transformation, of course, stems from the most profound change in society of the century just gone: women who work. My grandmother knitted and over-boiled cabbage and looked after her husband. My mother abandoned work for marriage and children — though her cabbage was always crisp and bicarbonate-of-soda green. My wife's mother, a really high-flying civil servant, was given the specific choice of her love or her job. Grandparents, in such circumstances, were remote appendages — grave idols to be visited to a rota but not to be involved in the upbringing of the next generation.

Today, as a matter of basic practicality, such divides don't work. The mother and the father of the grandchildren work. If they're lucky in life, they can afford a full-time nanny; if they're not, going to work necessarily involves a hectic schedule of mindings and deliverings. Either way, the grandparents can't be non-combatants. They are the cavalry just over the hill when things go wrong. They are the support team of first — and last — resort. And that's terrific because, in an odd way, it puts a new element of family back into family life. Indeed, in some cases, in some families, it produces an entirely changed definition of what family life means.

My third grandson — now a year and a bit — has a Spanish passport. He was born in a Barcelona hospital while his Galician dad looked on. And, diving off the Easyjet, running up the stairs to the third floor, I caught a glimpse of another way which

17

may be becoming our way. No wards. They carried little Leonardo back to a separate (NHS) room with a bed for Dad, who slept there over five nights, changing the first nappies, taking turns at the most ordinary nursing duties, learning the things he'd need to know when baby came home. So much for Spanish machismo.

But, more than that, the whole emphasis was on involvement, family involvement. The floor wasn't anything like its British equivalent, with relatives and friends in desultory numbers pottering in and out. It was, throughout the day, a family hive of endeavour. The grandparents were first out of the blocks. They weren't merely welcome there; they were part of the fabric of the place, making it tick.

This hospital, mirroring the society it served, was about inclusion. Its society, one or many more generations back, was a village society, in which everybody had their place and role. So it was here. No spare parts. And my son-in-law's mother is living proof of that. Her Galician village is lost miles in the depths of that wild, green province, up a dirt track and far from the metalled road. She kept the family and the farm going while her husband roamed the coal mines and the cornfields looking for work. "Are you going to breast-feed?" she asked my daughter once. "Good. That is so much more practical. You can draw water from the well or get the cows in at the same time."

I'm not, of course, suggesting that Britain 2000 is becoming the undiscovered Spain of decades past;

but there is a hard-headed sense of duty to the situation, I begin to discover. It is the way we are coming to live now. It probably won't last (for reasons beyond the shaping of politicians), but while it endures it offers something new and pretty wonderful: the possibility of families bound together in the tasks of caring and rearing over generations.

Won't last? Why on earth not, if it's so desirable? Beyond the reach of politicians? Can't they fix everything? Let me explain. The things I've been describing are not just random and individual. They are part of the pattern of how we live, and the pattern changes. Maybe slowly, so we don't realize it, but change comes none the less. Consider: neither the grandmothers I had, nor the mother or mother-in-law, had a job outside the home. Child-raising was the job they did. If they had a career before marriage, they were obliged to throw it in.

Now, a couple of generations on, that normality is almost precisely reversed. Unions bargain anxiously about the terms of maternity leave. Europe insists on paternity leave. The prevailing reality assumes a mother and father both working. The explosion of women's rights has made that possible. The growth of a more sophisticated consumer society — with mortgages to pay and holidays to plan — has made this a necessity, the underpinning of modern society.

Here is where grandparents, according to this thesis, fit in. Here, also, is the reason for the helter-skelter expansion of homes for the elderly when they grow too frail to be part of the functioning family unit. Fifty years back they would have stayed much longer with their son or daughter in a true home — because the wife kept open house twenty-four hours a day. Now she has a career of her own, and the whole financial edifice depends on keeping it going.

Other things are changing in tandem. You know what Social Security ministers say (irrespective of party). The population of Britain is ageing. The old are living longer. The burden of pension provision in the welfare state simply cannot be allowed to continue far into the next century because the burden on those in work — the ones who create the wealth — is too great. Therefore, through our working lives we have somehow to set more aside to tide us through the years of retirement.

What these ministers don't always say, however, is that the population is ageing not just because of better health and living longer but because fewer babies are being born. Britain isn't replacing its generations as they pass away. It is shrinking as well as ageing on every current trend, and it is by no means alone: the birth rate in most of mainland Europe is even lower. By the time my Spanish grandson hits fifty, there will (according to the best United Nations figures) be 8 million fewer Spaniards. Italy, Germany and Greece are shrivelling too.

Good news for an overcrowded planet? Not within the boundaries of nations like ours if we wish to hang on to the normalities of our existence. This is a real problem, steaming over the horizon. And the reasons behind it are some of the reasons why change keeps pounding on. A world where both men and women work is a world where there is less time and less inclination to have a big family. Children tend increasingly to come along later in the life cycle, after the wife or partner has established herself in a career. So there are fewer children. They arrive, when they do, in a home and a lifestyle conditioned by years of two salaries coming in. Kids are expensive. They demand financial sacrifice. But the sacrifice tends to be made less and less readily. And so the spiral continues.

Here's the sadness to go with my new happy state, the chill wind of impending transition. We — the new generation of grandparents — are the lucky ones. The pensions crisis hasn't quite happened. The fashion for early retirement gives us many more active years. Our children, and their children, need us. The second career, in part, is a return to family service.

But reality is biting away at this condition. Already in France, as the age crunch comes, the retirement age is going up to seventy, and Britain is sure to follow suit. As our sons and daughters postpone the time when they pause to make babies, the years we will have to get to know our grandchildren, and to be useful to them, are diminishing apace. The wheels whirl on.

Meanwhile, here I sit, a modern Werther Original. Not telling dusty fairy stories to the four-year-old at my side and feeding him teeth-rotting toffees but teaching him to work my computer so that one day soon he can teach me things. Granny bounds about with renewed purpose. She knows about nappy rash and temperatures and sleeping habits. She's been there and done all that. She has the wisdom of experience to impart. Her relations with her children and the wives and husbands have shifted on to a totally unprophesied footing — that of the unpaid, but respected, professional consultant.

Do we — the new consultants — get all the advice we need? Not really. Advertising and publishing are still locked in the time warp of a youth market which is bailing out on them. Grandmothers may rate a few books of bromide advice; grandfathers are still the great unadvised in woolly cardigans, stuffing sweets or swinging golf clubs. But our time — our all too brief time — has come.

I had, in an inchoate way, feared the moment when the office doors began to close. You'd had the great good fortune to be part of a shared enterprise, a working community, and now that was coming to a close. The world beyond looked ominously devoid of signposts. But the world we have, at least for the moment, is a world of opportunity as well as loss and regret. It has structured itself, almost by accident, to offer a life after conventional work which is a return to the life of two or three decades ago, when you were an umbilical part of the family.

Regrets? Of course. That I probably won't be there when the four-year-old becomes the next Bill Gates. But meanwhile his tiny fingers on the keys have a message of their own. And my fingers are there, too, pressing the button marked Enter.

JEAN REID

Squaring the social circle

We were in Glasgow, finishing a leisurely lunch, enjoying the spring sunshine on the patio of a West End café, when things began to click into place. Our conversation had sauntered along various pathways, touching on auld acquaintance and new homes, families and the world situation, when my friend tossed in the casual inquiry, "How do you meet new people?"

"Funny you should ask me that," I replied, pointing out that the question had dominated my waking hours ever since I had decided it was too late to turn down the assignment to write this piece — a sort of contract by inertia. The past week or so had been spent on a series of false starts as it became increasingly clear that my views on getting a social life were of little use to anyone — at best pompous, at worst patronizing.

Funnier still was that the question should come from Vee, a person whose social skills had left me open-mouthed on many occasions. Within minutes of meeting someone new she had a knack of finding some link — a common acquaintance, familiar place or shared enthusiasm — which kept the conversation flowing and established rapport. And it was all done with an innocent interest which disarmed any accusations of intrusion or vulgar curiosity. If I tried the same it tended to sound like interrogation. Besides, I'm always a bit leery of stumbling across long-held grudges or sensitive spots — I have a tendency to spot the pitfall just as my foot lands in it.

My friendship with Vee went back almost thirty years, though I had hardly seen her for the past twenty. We met on the deck of a fishing boat heading for Scotland's most remote island with an assorted party of volunteers. We started to chat, and almost immediately she identified one good friend, several acquaintances and a number of interests we had in common. Two weeks of bird-watching, sheep-counting, dyke-repairing and spartan living cemented the bond, despite a significant (at that stage) age gap.

For a year or two our circles overlapped in a succession of outings, parties and reunions with other St Kilda veterans. Then her marriage and my change of job rearranged the pattern. I visited Vee just once in her Hebridean home, but the contact lapsed into the occasional Christmas card or message passed on by shared friends. Yet here we were, chatting away as if the past quarter-century had no more distancing effect than a long weekend. It made me wonder just where friendship fits into

25

social life — is it simply the sum of the people you know or something quite different?

I count myself lucky in the range of friends I have made — and retained — over the decades. Some I scarcely see from one year's end to the next, though we keep in touch by phone or card; my social life, on the other hand, involves lots of people I would class as friendly acquaintances, folk I'm pleased to meet and talk to but wouldn't normally visit or invite to a party.

Since I've spent all but a few years of my life in or near my native city, it's not surprising that I see familiar faces wherever I go. The fact that more people seem to recognize me than vice versa is not a sign of local fame: I have always suffered from a kind of facial dyslexia which often delays identification till the early hours of the morning ("Of course, that's who it was!"). Even with the prompting of a name I can't always place a schoolmate who recalls where I sat in the maths class or one of my jokier remarks.

Such a stable — let's admit it, unenterprising — background would suggest that my social life would revolve round the family and friends of my youth. Not so: I feel no real sense of belonging at our occasional school reunions, and the student friends I keep up with are scattered around the length and breadth of Scotland. Apart from celebrations and crises, I don't expect to see family on a regular basis. Ironically, the ones I know best are the farthest flung.

So why should I be pontificating about social life? Reports of mine have been greatly exaggerated. It's true that I go out a lot, mainly to meetings or vaguely cultural events where I'm often greeted with remarks like "What a busy life you lead, you must go to everything" — from people who don't seem to have noticed that they must also be there to have seen me. Maybe they too have decided that the telly is rubbish and the washing can wait (any excuse), and anyway they'd like to see what the fuss is about or have promised this or that producer or performer or whoever to attend.

But I'm usually on my own, not because I'm particularly anti-social but often because it's a last-minute decision. Besides, I have learned over the years that no company is far better than a companion who is palpably bored or disapproving or possibly even asleep. So for plays, films and concerts I seldom search for a partner, though I'm usually happy enough to fit in with any suggestions from others. They can then take the blame if it proves a disaster. Through innumerable amateur and community shows, as well as many an overlong professional performance, I have acquired a high level of tolerance: I'm almost unshiftable once I've got my bum firmly planted on a seat — it's my greatest contribution to the arts.

Maybe I am a bit of a loner, after all. Always have been, when I think of it — not someone who has kept a "best friend" since nursery school days through all the traumas of adolescence and maturity. I've had my best friends from time to time, but more often my circle has revolved round an inner group of three or four, not always the same people.

Those of my contemporaries who took the conventional route through marriage and children (in my youth they went strictly together) acquired not only an immediate family but lasting friends through shared experience — of childbirth, babysitters, nursery groups, parent-teacher associations, teenage angst, empty nests and now grandchildren. This is, of course, fine while it lasts but can be devastating when a partner is lost or the next generation flits to the other side of the world.

Inevitably, my social circle is made up mainly of other independent souls who are rather less tied to domesticity — though more and more now find their activities constrained by cats or gardens or both. They tend to be around my own age or up to a generation less, while a surprising number have no young relatives. I rejoice in a growing clutch of great-nephews and nieces, widespread enough to ensure that every get-together is a treat.

Many of these friends are survivors from a succession of intersecting circles. There are the student contacts, kindred spirits from group holidays, past flatmates and colleagues, people I've worked with on various projects. Most of us share interests in the arts and environment and have a roughly similar attitude to social questions, and we all enjoy putting the world to rights over a good meal and a glass or two. But we don't live in one another's pockets, and there may be little or no contact for weeks, or even years, on end.

What I must admit is that none of my close friends, as distinct from acquaintances, have been acquired in the ways usually recommended by agony aunts. The favourite used to be: "Join a tennis club", but, since I gave up playing at the age of twelve when I couldn't find anyone bad enough to match me, that was obviously out. Later on, the advice was to "go to an evening class". I did try that in my twenties with some success in the circle-building field, but later a succession of time-absorbing jobs kept me busy enough to avoid making choices.

That's not to say that I didn't join things. Indeed, for one who shares Groucho Marx's doubts about having anything to do with a club which would accept him, I've been a member of a surprising number of organizations for decades. Usually that's because I've wanted to support what they were trying to do rather than from any real wish to get involved, and in a depressing number of cases I've shared in the obsequies for societies which have reached the end of their useful life.

While some organizations have certainly added to my circle of good acquaintances, that has always been a by-product: if I'd gone looking for them it wouldn't have worked. In my experience, social life cannot be manufactured, though it can be helped along by taking the trouble to host a meeting or throw the odd party. So the message, if there must be one, is to follow your genuine interests and accept all promising invitations; otherwise, leave it to fate. As you'll have gathered, I'm a drifter at heart.

Three years or so after giving up gainful employment I still haven't found time for any of the worthwhile pursuits I promised myself — learning a language, completing the West Highland Way, sampling other people's pleasures such as bingo or the races, researching my ancestors, even the odd good work. Since I'm hopeless at fund-raising, which is what many worthy causes seem most interested in, my only contribution to date has been a regular half-day in a charity shop. This has added more to my wardrobe than my social circle, though it does give shape to the week and I am developing my till skills.

So far, my increased leisure had been frittered away on long lunches, film matinées, crosswords, the odd outdoor expedition (usually with a bit of persuasion from more energetic friends), wee naps in the afternoon, getting to know existing friends better, small bits of reorganization — all my photographs are now in albums, recipes have been sorted into categories. The dry rot has been tackled and the kitchen remodelled — pity I still can't find time for anything but the most perfunctory cleaning when I have readjusted my timetable so that visitors can be expected.

I've dabbled in oils in a painting group run by my near-contemporary dance teacher, a friend of a friend who is the hub of several lively social circles. I've been talked on to committees where my main contribution is to ask awkward questions or perhaps put together a bit of prose for publication. And I've gone to openings, parties and events whenever I'm invited or feel inclined — it's always a chance to stay in touch.

Sad to say I haven't yet established contact with my Best Friend — as defined by British Telecom — but I'm hoping to find my way back into the internet before too long, with a bit of help. Meanwhile I'm making good use of the word processor to list all sorts of things, from books to contents of cupboards; maybe in time I'll get round to my life story.

One of my false starts to these meanderings drew a rather precious parallel between the look of a lived-in face and a person's social life: the lines were pretty well set by middle age and would simply deepen and spread as time went on. That wasn't to say that social contacts, like facial features, could not be improved by judicious dollops of TLC and gentle massaging of egos. But, barring accident or strenuous effort, the pattern would not change dramatically.

And maybe that holds good for socializing: if the habit has been established, you'll be able to adapt the smile of welcome to altered circumstances, however traumatic. I can think, for instance, of widows who have taken up new activities, such as hill-walking and painting, and through them found not only an absorbing interest but also a brand new social circle.

So where does this all take us? Back to my friend, Vee, perhaps. Her question was not, as it may have read, a plea for advice, simply an inquiry into the process as I saw it. Her reappearance in my life was brought about by two factors — the couple's return to the mainland and their student children's move to my part of the world.

Vee had come through to tidy up the back yard of their basement flat. Typically she had met more of their neighbours in a couple of days than I had got to know in eight years. But she was also contemplating a move back to old haunts and wondering how long it would take her to build up a new circle of congenial folk. Knowing Vee, I'd say a month at the outside.

KURT STRAUSS

Cheveux gris, éminence grise?

It takes chutzpah to ring your friends and invite them to contribute their thoughts on the ageing process from their own personal experience. "Me? Old? Never!" Well, actually yes, and sooner than some of us think. Only fairy-tale characters live happily, or for that matter unhappily, ever after. In the real world old age is upon us before we know it. It was certainly upon me before I knew it. Looking back, I can remember quite clearly the day it tapped me on the shoulder and said: "You're past it, Kurt, old chap", or words to that effect. "It" had taken on the form of my boss, and what "it" actually said was: "How would you like to take early retirement?" "Me? Retire? Never!"

I hadn't even reached my three score, never mind the extra ten which the actuaries of the Old Testament suggested as being an average figure for life expectancy. But apparently the company had someone younger in mind to take over from me, a colleague whom I knew well and whose department

I once had visions of incorporating into my own. And now the converse was being suggested. Definitely a χ, I thought.

"Ah, but there's a generous severance package," went on my boss and produced an envelope on the back of which someone in Personnel had scribbled a few figures, all of which had a number of noughts behind them. "Mmmm," I said, "I'll take it home and think about it." Well, that evening, sitting in front of my pocket calculator (only big firms and rich people could afford a computer in those days), I did some sums, added some figures, took away the number I had first thought of (i.e. the pension I would get were I to stay on till sixty-five) and decided that perhaps I was looking at a $\sqrt{}$ after all.

To cut a long story short, I took the money and ran ... and I've been running ever since. Well, walking briskly, anyway. Oh, all right; I do sometimes slow down to a leisurely stroll, but then I'm not as young as I was, you know. So there's a χ and a $\sqrt{}$ straight away, the χ being the loss of a job which I had greatly enjoyed doing and the $\sqrt{}$ being paid for not doing it.

All in all, my old age (I suppose I have to accept that as a "given") seems to have its sprinkling of χ and $\sqrt{}$ and they are manifest in roughly equal measure. Take, as an example, the hours of darkness, when most people like to have a good night's sleep. Indeed, we oldsters positively need a good night's sleep. But do we get one?

χ Do we heck. At some time between 1 and 3a.m. we wake up and realize that we can either make a dash for the toilet now this instant or go back to sleep and risk waking up later on a damp piece of bed-linen. Me, I tend to chicken out and go for the loo, trying hard not to wake up more than I have to in the process so that with any luck I can get back to bed and back to sleep without too much difficulty. Happily this often proves to be the case, but then the whole scenario is repeated some hours later, when it's no longer so easy not to awaken fully. Why? Because dawn is approaching. In fact, those blessed hours of darkness are getting shorter by the day, but . . . hey:

√ That must be a sign that spring is on the way, with summer not far behind and, besides, who needs to get up in the morning? Not us old ones √. And if I feel the need of a short doze in the afternoon no one will hold it against me; certainly not my boss, seeing as how I don't have any boss but myself. Just a minute, though; there's a √ side to this matter of being bossless and unemployed. If I'm my own boss, I'm actually self-employed and pretty busy with it. Now,

χ My understanding of the national minimum wage, maximum hours, paid sick leave, statutory holidays and so on is that they don't apply to the self-employed any more than to the unemployed. We oldies never get a day off, now I come to think of it. Whereas weekends used to be something to look forward to, and the journey to work during the week an opportunity to read the paper, old age has deprived me of both these pleasures and a number of others. For me, now, Sunday is the day the milkman doesn't come, and that's almost the only way to recognize it, church-going apart. The shops are open, and the traffic is just as thick, if not thicker . . .

√ Actually I don't have to shop when the rest of the world does, nor do I have to wait till the weekend to visit my friends, most of whom are as old as I am and so benefit from the same freedom to decide how to use their time. And as for not reading the paper, I'm saving pounds every week by not buying one √ and don't have to worry about (a) not having enough time to read it all and (b) recycling it and the dozens of wretched supplements I didn't want and didn't ask for anyway.

With twenty-five or more other people writing in this little volume about so many other aspects of being old in Britain today, it behoves me not to trespass on what might be their patch, but then again, as I sometimes think to myself when cycling the wrong way up a one-way street, what's wrong with a bit of trespass? Or other gentle law-breaking? Laws are there to be tested, and who better to test them than us old people? The public thinks nothing of it if a young hooligan is fined for defacing a wall with graffiti, but it takes an old hooligan spraying something like "BAN GMOs NOW" on the Ministry of Agriculture, Fisheries and Food building or "TROOPS OUT OF IRAQ" on the

Ministry of Defence's pavement in Whitehall to arouse some interest. The police will be somewhat reluctant to arrest an eighty-year-old granny, especially if the press and TV cameramen are there to record the event. We old folk can behave pretty outrageously and often get away with it, though "outrageously" is probably not the correct adjective to apply — "eccentrically" might be better. There are limits, of course. However old I am, it wouldn't do to drive the wrong way up a motorway, as some folk try to do — and not just the old and forgetful.

χ Forgetfulness is one of the big of old age, without a doubt. A good friend of mine confesses to having a forgettery where her memory used to be, and this can be anything from inconvenient ("Where did I put my glasses?") through embarrassing ("I'm sorry, who did you say you were?") to downright dangerous ("I'm awfully sorry, officer. I could have sworn I was in the right carriageway. I did, though, wonder about all those cars hurtling past in the other direction"). The trick here is to train yourself to forget the nasty bits, and I don't mean appointments with the dentist. "Was that weekend/film/party/dish/holiday really so dreadful? I'd quite forgotten."

√ I find I am quite popular with people who enjoy telling stories, or jokes, or any of the other things one tells (I'm sorry; I can't remember what they are), because in me they have the perfect audience. No matter how often they've already told me, I'm wide-eyed and open-mouthed at every new, or as it might be not-so-new, telling. And I don't worry any more about my inability to recognize names, faces or both, happy in the knowledge that because I am old they will forgive me my trespasses √.

There's something else alongside memory loss, and that's hair, tooth, hearing and eyesight loss, never mind stamina, mobility, suppleness and libido loss. I remember another elderly friend telling me, as she fished around for her spectacles and her hearing aid, that one of the signs of old age is that you have to carry your senses around in your handbag. If you can remember where you put it, that is. I myself don't yet have such problems, partly because I don't carry a handbag but mainly because I still have most of my own teeth, never take off my specs (except to go to sleep), hear moderately well (if people remember to speak up) and still have enough hair for the world to see that it is a fine shade of grey. As is my beard. In the Far East, grey hair and grey beards count for something, so I'm told.

√ Old age brings with it an aura of *éminence grise* and *cheveux gris*, things that help to convey that impression of sage counsel. When young striplings come to you for advice, you can stroke your beard and say, "Well, now . . ." and after due reflection tell them what course of action they should pursue. Not everyone wants to grow a beard, of course. Older women in particular might find such things difficult, moustaches being bad enough. In my case, though, it was the obvious thing to do following the catastrophic failure of an electric razor while on holiday several miles from the nearest electric razor repair facility. To begin with, this was seen as a calamity of major proportion, but gradually I came to realize that by not shaving I could have an extra three minutes in bed in the mornings √.

There then arose some anxiety about foreign travel. What would the immigration officers say when my face no longer corresponded with my mugshot? Would I be denied entry or exit from the country I was hoping to enter or re-enter? But no, all was well. Indeed, when I considered shaving it off again many years later, thinking that I might thereby contrive to make myself look younger, my wife insisted that I should do no such thing. She had got used to it, she said — nay, she had become fond of it, so it had to stay.

χ The trouble is, the British Isles are not the Far East, and the younger generations, far from revering their elders and betters, more often deride them, ignore them or at worst turn against them. "What do you know about it, Granddad?" they say, and sadly I have to admit that the answer is: "Nothing." Be it the Brit Awards contenders, the Performance Artists, the Football Supporters or the Trainspotters, I have to confess that their language is not my language, their tastes are not my tastes and their values are not, as a rule, my values.

The world is passing me by χ and, though I'm old, I'm not old enough yet to stop it and get off. So I walk down my high street where the fast-food outlet has replaced the grocery store, the chrome-plated coffee bar stands where Wendy's once served afternoon tea and the mode boutique offers minuscule garments for megapound prices. And in the evening I sit in front of my television set, wondering how to set the video to record the programme that won't start till long after my bedtime. On the other hand, though,

√ There's a video shop in the high street where the butcher's used to be, and I couldn't help but notice a rather fetching cover picture on one of the cassettes as I went past. I wonder what it costs to hire it. And the public library will actually lend them √ out. Of course, I have to get there first, but if I don't travel before 9.30a.m. (as if I would!) I can use my free travel pass √ and the chances are that someone will take one look at my grey hair and offer me a seat √ and I know a little place where they do smashing meals at special rates for OAPs √ and, talking of OAPs, most cinemas, theatres, museums, galleries and so forth have concessionary rates √ and . . . maybe old age isn't so bad after all √ √ √.

The last word on the subject of old age should, I think, be with Father William, whom I've held in high regard ever since he was introduced to me by Lewis Carroll. The whole of this splendid man's exchange with his insufferable son is worth quoting, but space doesn't allow it, so I'll just recall the start of the poem:

"You are old, Father William," the young man said,
"And your hair has become very white;
And yet you incessantly stand on your head —
Do you think, at your age, it is right?"
"In my youth," Father William replied to his son,
"I feared it might injure the brain;
But now that I'm perfectly sure I have none,
Why, I do it again and again."

TAKING STOCK

Claire Rayner

Monty Meth

Vera Ivers

Paulette Bauckham

Ivor Smith-Cameron

Gillian Ford

CLAIRE RAYNER

Exclusion and inclusion

"Social exclusion" is one of the phrases of our times, along with other little gems like the institutionalized "isms" (first applied to racism and the police force, later to ageism and the NHS, with no doubt a reference to out-of-townism and the supermarkets just over the horizon) and "New Labour". What they have in common is a certain haziness about their meaning. I shan't attempt here to consider just what an institutionalized "ism" is, nor the actual meaning of the New Labour label; that belongs to another day in another place. It is the notion of social exclusion that I find interesting, because I reckon I've been socially excluded for most of my life, one way or another.

First of all, I was born into poverty — and I mean real poverty. In 1931 the selection of teenage parents, living hand to mouth in the East End of London, was not the choice of an intelligent infant. Secondly, I was born Jewish, again an unwise option at a time when anti-Semitism was the norm. Both of these meant I was excluded from a considerable area of British social life which took in the well fed, the well housed, the well shod.

More exclusion was to come. Being a Londoner meant that when the war started and I was eight years old and it was deemed necessary to send children away from the risk of German bombs I became an evacuee. And I am here to tell you that there is no social exclusion as thoroughly excluding as being a town child, and a poor Jewish one to boot, in your average English village.

We move on to the late forties, when I reached my teen years. Teenagers hadn't been invented then — they didn't really appear in the UK until the mid-1950s or thereabouts — so I was part of that uneasy bunch of socially excluded people who were neither children nor adults. Then, when I did at last achieve adulthood and began to think that maybe I could be regarded as having earned the right to join the human race, lo and behold, I discovered that my gender excluded me from all sorts of things. Like being a medical student at the same time as being married. I had to choose one or the other. (Feminism? What's that?)

And so it has gone on. Having chosen to be a young wifeandmother (have you never noticed that it is one word?) I was excluded from the world of work and earning; until I got mad and decided I'd do both, no matter what society said about mothers who had the temerity to think they had the right to a life of their own outside the walls of the nursery and the kitchen and went after a career. Which immediately catapulted me into yet another socially excluded group, the Working Mother.

I have now joined another couple of socially excluded groups: the elderly and the disabled. Numerate readers will have worked out that I'm well into my late sixties — well into my pensioned years — and I'm also lame (some pretty extensive orthopaedic surgery following a fall has left me with limited mobility) and more than a little deaf.

So, do I warrant attention from Tony Blair's Social Exclusion Unit, based at the Cabinet Office to take care of all us outsiders? I don't think I do. Because when I look back over the years at the various sections of society from which I've been excluded, I realize something very obvious that I have totally missed until now: that being excluded from one group means that I have been automatically included in others. I belonged very closely indeed to that tight-knit — almost claustrophobically so — world of East End Jewry. I belonged to the equally tight desperately-clinging-together children who were the "vaccies". I belonged to that union of women — mothers of young children — finding friends and fellow nappy-changers everywhere I went. And now there is an army of slightly deaf, lame oldies in whose ranks I feel very much at home.

And there is an important point to be remembered: I was not always pushed into or excluded from these various groupings involuntarily. There was an element of choice in my adult years. I chose to opt for wifeandmother rather than medical student. I decided of my own free will to be a Working Mum. I took silly risks that resulted in the fall that injured my knees and led to the surgery that left me with diminished mobility. Surely the same may be true for other people?

For example, consider those young people who opt for a life as squatters or living as hand-to-mouth beggars. Think of some older people who live on the streets, under makeshift tents and in cardboard boxes. Contemplate those elderly recluses who live in rooms piled high with old newspapers, assorted junk collected over many years, a number of cats and no other human beings. Many sage and deeply sad nods will greet such definitions, no doubt — but not from thoughtful people. They will wonder whether the people who live that way have been forced to do so, as a result of being drummed out of the wider community of people who pay rent and have jobs, or whether they have chosen to live as they do.

After all, no one ever uses the "socially excluded" label for people who live in gated estates of large houses surrounded by high fences complete with anti-intruder alarms and with dour, burly blokes in uniforms manning gatehouses. It is taken for granted that they have chosen to stand aloof from the rest of the world, preferring the company of people like themselves.

It may be true that the majority of people opt for being like everyone else and living lives that follow a mutually agreed (if never formally written) code that involves ordinary jobs, ordinary lifestyles and ordinary aspirations, but there are many who want anything but ordinary lives. They despise the code and all who live by it. Describing this latter group as excluded is to be exceedingly arrogant. They resigned, dammit, from a group they didn't choose to be in.

If you are one of those people who resent being labelled as an older person, think again. What is the alternative? To be one of that huge group labelled "dead"?

That certainly wouldn't be my choice. If there is one thing I have discovered as I've wandered through the various groups which have claimed me as a member, it is that for all I may be losing by not being part of a different, maybe bigger and richer one, the one I'm in has something to offer that is special, enjoyable and that I wouldn't be without. Thus, as an elderly, lame, somewhat deaf person, I'm enjoying the freedom of having reached the age of indiscretion. I can say what I like and do what I like, and indulgent society (well, quite a chunk of it) will put it down to my age and condition and make no fuss at all. Bliss!

MONTY METH

The best is yet to come

Like so many others of my generation I came into a world where discrimination loomed large in my formative years. Opposing it, albeit at different times and in different situations, remains very much a part of my daily agenda.

Today my primary concern is with ageism in its various forms, but my earliest experience was of racial discrimination before the Second World War — being set on as a schoolboy by a gang of fascist bullies while walking down Hackney Road in London's East End, where I then lived. Later I was confronted with a different form of discrimination because the youth club to which I belonged was exclusively for Jewish boys. Jewish girls had a separate club, and the non-Jewish lads with whom we went to school and played in the streets of Bethnal Green were barred.

That was until January 1938 when, after a fierce debate among leaders of the Association of Jewish Youth, the Cambridge and Bethnal Green Jewish Boys' Club was allowed, despite the misgivings of many other club leaders, to drop the "Jewish" from its name and become a non-sectarian club. By the end of 1938 it had 320 Jewish lads and 80 non-Jewish members — some of whom remain my friends to this day.

Though no objections were received from Jewish parents of club members, Jewish community leaders were strongly opposed to the desegregation plan and my mentors, the brothers George and Roland Lotinga, who led the challenge to the practice of boys from different faiths being in different clubs, had to defend their "alarming suggestion" before such leading Jewish luminaries as Basil Henriques and Neville Laski.

The Lotingas were almost certainly influenced in their opposition to all-Jewish youth clubs by the events in Nazi Germany and the fascist activities on their doorstep in Bethnal Green. In February 1938 the *Jewish Chronicle* sat on the fence and viewed a youth club opening its doors to boys of any religion as a matter "of deep concern to all interested in the club movement". But by December 1938 it was compelled to note that the experiment is "working out very well".

Today it seems hard to believe that opposition to this ending of discrimination by a solitary boys' club in East London could attract so much attention and cause so much controversy — and not all of it within the Jewish community. A then leader of the London Federation of Boys' Clubs, W. McG. Eager, a Christian youth worker, was not convinced by the

Cambridge and Bethnal Green experience, adding that "common membership without a common religious basis and social tradition lacks moral justification".

My youthful arguments about assimilation, social tensions and integration certainly helped to prepare me for the world of work when, as Industrial Correspondent of the *Daily Mail* in the late 1960s, I was asked by the Runnymede Trust, an independent research body specializing in race relations, to write two booklets on the racial situation in British industry.

The *Daily Mail* of those days was not as enlightened as it has been lately over the Stephen Lawrence murder, and there was some embarrassment that these booklets, called *Here to Stay* and *Brothers to All Men?*, challenged the attitudes and discriminatory practices of both employers and the trade unions towards Britain's labour force — then estimated to include some 750,000 coloured workers. But I soon learned that you couldn't write about race relations in industry in the 1970s without ruffling a few feathers.

Trade union leaders, in particular, who claimed they were "colour-blind" or said that they were "unaware of any racial problems whatever", did not like their "all men are brothers" philosophy being publicly challenged to face the real world of racial discrimination in industry. So it is good to see that twenty years later both unions and employers in general now no longer adopt a leave-it-alone line but, rather, have a more open approach in implementing positive and constructive policies.

Battling and winning the fight against discrimination certainly takes time and patience, as I have learned from my experience working with the Carnegie United Kingdom Trust for the past ten years. The trust has played a pioneering role in combating discrimination on two fronts — disability and ageism — and I have been privileged in being allowed to help some of the most wonderful community-minded people who are completely dedicated to the service of others.

For many years the Carnegie UK Trust had sought to expose discrimination against disabled people, who were being virtually barred from enjoying visits to theatres, cinemas, concert halls, museums and art galleries because of the lack of facilities such as ramps for wheelchair users, toilets for disabled people and hearing systems. The trust produced reports unmasking the disgraceful treatment handed out to disabled people and undertook surveys of the facilities in, for example, theatres in London's West End and cinemas in Scotland. The almost universal answer was that to treat disabled people as equal patrons was too costly.

So to its eternal credit Carnegie and its secretary, Geoffrey Lord, in particular, agreed to call the bluff of venue owners, local authorities and government. It decided to create the charity ADAPT — Access for Disabled People to Arts Premises Today — which offered incentive grants to any organization that would end the discrimination against disabled people who were — and in some cases still are — deprived of seeing and enjoying the arts in all its many forms alongside the rest of us.

Our case was, of course, unanswerable. There were grants from some corporate givers as well as the trust itself, and we even prised money out of the then Heritage and Arts Ministry to enable us to name and shame the venues blocking entry to disabled people. Just thinking about two examples of that anti-discrimination campaign still makes me angry: seeing disabled people demonstrating at cinemas that refused them entry to see the prize-winning film *My Left Foot*, whose hero is himself disabled with cerebral palsy; and hearing of a Scottish cinema complex which built a toilet for disabled people but where to reach it disabled women had to go through the men's toilet.

It was cases like these that made us campaign all the harder for justice for disabled people, and when the National Lottery came along Carnegie had one of its biggest victories when it persuaded the government that no lottery grants should be made to arts venues unless they included provision for disabled people.

ADAPT was launched in 1989 at the same time that the trust embarked on probably its biggest-ever project — the Carnegie Inquiry into the Third Age. This was the first inquiry in the world to probe the impact on society of the increase in life expectancy, the changing pattern of work and healthier living.

As we all now know, people today can in general look forward to another twenty or thirty years of active life after they have finished their main full-time career, or rearing a family, or both.

But in 1989 it took a trade union leader and an industrialist — two men normally expected to be on opposite sides of the table — to recognize that big changes were taking place in the life and work patterns of older people. The Carnegie UK Trust had the good fortune to have these two people of vision among its trustees: Lionel Murray, now Lord Murray, the former TUC General Secretary, and Sir Timothy Colman, Chairman of the Eastern Counties Newspaper Group and a former director of Reckitt and Colman. Together with Geoffrey Lord they went to see the highly respected author, adviser and management expert Charles Handy, who confirmed that there was indeed something new emerging and agreed that the future of work was worth probing together with its related issues.

This inquiry reported in 1993, and since that year we have come from a position where nobody — politicians and the media in particular — wanted to discuss the third age to one where a Better Government for Older People project has been run out of the Cabinet Office, a new deal for older people seeking work has been promised for the over-fifties with cash employment credits and a training subsidy, an inter-ministerial group on older people has been set up, and there have been numerous other initiatives to encourage them to act as volunteers or participate in lifelong learning opportunities.

When the Carnegie Inquiry warned that the state pension was being allowed to wither away because increases were being tied to price rises and not to average earnings, or when it reported that there was discrimination against older people in getting NHS treatment, hardly anybody out there wanted to listen. A wall of silence was erected by those who did not want to recognize the new phenomenon called the third age in which millions of fit, active, healthy and independent people are seeking a new role in society.

My current and probably last battle is still alongside the Carnegie UK Trust — against age discrimination in employment. This is a campaign that will not go away because it strikes at the heart of so many aspects of our daily lives. How is it possible, I ask myself, that nearly 40 per cent of seven-year-old children cannot read and 7 million adults are unable to read a telephone directory — yet MPs are bombarded with letters from forty-year-old teachers who cannot get jobs? No wonder there is an organization in Britain called the Association of Teachers Against Ageism.

How is it possible for the Treasury to argue that work is the most important route out of poverty when only two-fifths of men aged between fifty-five and sixty-five are working? And of those that lose their jobs after fifty-five, only 11 per cent get another job? And how is it possible for ministers to talk about joined-up government and yet not see the obvious link between poverty and the fact that as many as 800,000 more men over fifty would be working today if the job opportunities for them had not declined? Or that one in fifteen men now aged forty-five to forty-nine may never work again or that of those currently unemployed as many as a half may never find another job?

Excluding so many people from work through compulsory or voluntary early retirement, or age discrimination, must reduce the funds available to government to increase the state pension, to provide long-term care for the older people or to fund better health, education and transport services.

Equally important, having some 3 million people over fifty registered as either unemployed or "economically inactive" must increase the burden on younger tax-payers and the government because so many people are making no contribution in income tax or in national insurance contributions to the pool from which state pensions and other services and benefits are paid.

It is because we see the clear and direct link between work and decent social services that so many of us are undoubtedly disappointed that the government has yet to redeem its pre-election pledge to end unjustifiable discrimination wherever it exists, let alone its pledge to make age discrimination in employment illegal — though Tony Blair has said it is still his policy. Meanwhile we are to be fobbed off until February 2001 with a non-statutory code of practice aimed at reducing age discrimination at work when everyone knows that this will not end the employment decline and fewer jobs for older people which has gone on for the past twenty years or more.

It may take a few more years to achieve, but I predict that we will yet see legislation against age discrimination on the statute book. Opposition to it will be overcome just as we have triumphed in our lifetime on so many other anti-discrimination issues — equal pay, race, sex and disability. That does not of course mean that we have eradicated prejudice, bias, bigotry and intolerance. But we "oldies" have taken some giant steps forward — and, I still believe, the best is yet to come.

VERA IVERS

A world still biased

One evening three of us, all women, met for a drink together. We have never been short of conversation and soon found ourselves discussing changes we had observed in our lives. We compared our lives to those of our daughters and wondered whether feminism had influenced the women we had become.

So, who were we? Well, first there was Joyce, who is sixty-six and who worked in a number of factories after leaving school at the age of fifteen. Two years later she married a man who turned out to be a drunkard who was violent towards her and their four children. Eventually she took the children and fled. She never remarried but has been in a happy relationship for ten years. To raise her children Joyce had to work very hard and did all manner of jobs, finally becoming a skilled machinist for a firm making women's fashionwear. She has now has eight grandchildren with whom she is very involved.

Then there was Annie. She is sixty-nine and married when she was twenty-two. She stayed at school until sixteen and then went to a further education college where she gained the required entry to teacher training. After a year at work she married and ceased to be a teacher. Later when her three children were at school she became an assistant in a day nursery and was then able to train as a nursery nurse. She is still married to the same man and has five grandchildren.

I was born in 1931, the eldest of five children, and, after my mother became very ill following the war, I spent many of my younger years caring for my brothers and sister. I first married at eighteen, and after that marriage broke down I eventually married again when I was forty-five. I have four children and two grandchildren. My first job was as junior in the office of a pickle factory and later I helped my dad on his fruit and flower stall. Much later I took up nursing, then moved on to social work while also serving on a local district and county council for seventeen years. My early education was scant, but when I was sixty-four I gained an MA by research.

All three of us experienced the 1939–45 war and the post-war period as girls and young women. That early part of our lives was spent in a world which mainly only recognized traditional lifestyles and relationships.

We all came from working-class families and enjoyed few privileges in terms of possessions, education or influence. But we considered ourselves lucky, because the communities into which we were born were close-knit and caring; not in a sentimental way but in terms of looking out for our safety and our upbringing. We were surrounded by strong women who offered us a model and what they saw as appropriate values. We learned about caring for the young and the old; we learned about housekeeping on a small budget. We learned about being respectable and respected and, most importantly, we learned how to keep our menfolk happy. Our mentors set great store by looking after the man and maintaining his authority and status in the family.

Though we all grew up with this model, we found it hilarious when talking it over in 1999. We realized from a very early age that it was the women who were the strong ones and it was they who made the decisions, while not upsetting the perceived order of things.

However, it was a serious requirement to uphold this vision of the strong authoritative man, even if we knew otherwise. I can remember very well my grandmother despairing of a neighbour of ours who felt let down by her husband. All the street would hear her ranting at him when he came home from work and would see the poor man hiding in his shed to get away from the endless criticisms. My gran worried about the children, who saw their father as weak and helpless. She said the children would end up in trouble because they had no man to look up to.

Annie had found a quote from John Stuart Mill in *The Subjection of Women* (published in 1869) and we thought the women in our families would have related to it absolutely. "Women", it said, "are declared to be better than men, an empty compliment which must provoke every woman with spirit, since there is no other situation in life in which it is the established order . . . that the better should obey the worst."

We all had memories of our mothers getting their own way without entering into confrontation with Father, and Annie gave us an example.

After the war people were beginning to think of making their homes more comfortable, and hire purchase was sometimes used to buy nice things. But it was still not quite respectable, and we could remember stories of families having their possessions removed when they couldn't keep up payments. Annie's dad was dead against "HP", but her mum desperately wanted to do up the front room so that she could ask people round for tea.

There was no use raising the subject with Dad, but she took him to visit everyone she knew who had a three-piece suite and never forgot to mention how nice it would be if they could ask them back. She brought the children into it by saying how much better it would be if they could bring their friends home. Dad soon came round, though at first he said they would have a nice front room when they had saved for it. It didn't take too long before Mum found such a good deal in a shop that he was persuaded to take on the dreaded HP, and of course every year it became more acceptable.

Joyce and I had left school at the earliest possible moment, even though I had gained a grant-aided place at a very prestigious girls' school. In later years I realized my mum had such different expectations from the school that it was never going to be a success. She wanted me to work in an office until I got married, instead of on the factory floor. The school, on the other hand, was interested in turning out brain surgeons and nuclear scientists.

It was not unusual for mothers to regard their daughters' future in terms of finding a husband who had a good trade or who could at least be relied on to bring home a steady wage. They would be more inclined to boast about a daughter who had managed such a catch than about one who was set on a long-term career. Annie's parents had been unusual in supporting her through further education. Mostly our families needed our wages as soon as possible.

We tried to remember what we had known about feminism and the women's movement when we were young. Not much was our conclusion. It was all going on while we were most burdened with work and family responsibilities. We certainly never attended any feminist meetings or read any literature. We knew more about the suffragette movement at the beginning of the century than the women's movement that followed it so much later.

I have often reflected on the way women were left out of important discussions in our family. I grew up in a house that was very involved with the labour movement. My mum was one of thirteen children, and her brothers were mostly dockers and involved in the emerging trade union movement. Gran's front room was used as a committee room for elections, and one of my uncles was a local councillor.

In such a world it was only the men who were involved in the world of unions and politics. Women delivered leaflets and made the tea, but my Auntie Jane, who always wanted to have a say in these events, was severely told off by Gran for poking her nose in where it wasn't wanted.

If feminism was discussed it wasn't named. And it was usually in the form of men reading bits from the tabloids about bra burning and lesbianism. Still, we realized that in spite of our early ignorance of the movement it had changed our lives; particularly in comparison with our mothers and grandmothers. Perhaps it is within relationships that the greatest changes have taken place.

Annie described her first days as a nursery nurse. It was always the mothers who delivered and fetched the children home. Now it is just as likely to be the fathers who undertake the nursery run, and they are sometimes even more enthusiastic about discussing their children's development. Annie could remember in her own family that her husband had been very proud of their children, but he would not be seen pushing the pram in case his mates saw him. Now, she says, he can't wait to take their grandson out in his pram and stops to let people admire him and discuss his progress.

We were not at all sure that women had entirely benefited from the greater opportunity to work outside the home. Men have recognized the need to help around the house, especially where women are working. However, our experience has been that they do not usually take responsibility for it. Women continue to be the mainstay of home and family, keeping everything organized and attending to the various needs.

Decisions in the home are more likely to made jointly now, though we could all recall our daughters quietly choosing to manipulate a decision rather than face an open challenge. This led to a lot of discussion, because in theory we could agree that women should by now feel confident enough to assert themselves and that subterfuge was not now justifiable. However, we were not absolutely sure, because we could all recall resorting to a bit of subterfuge from time to time.

In one area we felt there had been an immeasurable improvement. This was the way in which men were more likely to show their emotion now. Annie described her husband crying when he saw their first grandchild. She said she felt closer to him, because she was close to tears herself. We felt that such a show of emotion would not have happened in our parents' marriage or even in our own early days.

Women are still discriminated against when it comes to income and to services. We all had examples of men being offered more help from the service providers than women with similar disabilities or frailties. We were all worried about how we would pay for care when we became very old and felt this was a burden our mothers had not concerned themselves with. They were sure the family would take care of them and that, when that was not possible, the state would provide.

Recently I ran into a friend we all knew. She was looking very worn and tired and told me how much she has been involved in caring for her grandchildren, sometimes to a greater degree than she found easy. There was general agreement that young women often turned to their mothers for help with family and housekeeping. We understood their needs, because life was often very pressured for them. However, we thought that we could not have called on our mothers so often.

It was Joyce who offered the following thought for us to consider: "How did we become this generation in the middle? Our parents expected us to be around whenever they needed help, but we do not expect the same from our children. Instead we somehow expect to be on call for them whenever they need us."

It is not easy to conclude which of the changes that we have experienced in our lives has been due to the raising of a feminist voice. But we could all think of at least one major experience that seemed to have been the result of a move towards fairness and equality for women.

My first attempt to establish a career for myself came after an early marriage and children. I applied to be an auxiliary nurse in a hospital which was desperate for staff. It was a geriatric unit and of little interest to the young trained nurses at the time. The matron told me that she would accept me because she was so desperate. I tried to negotiate some conditions that would enable me to care for my children, but she stopped me in my tracks. "I do not agree with married women leaving their children merely for greed," she said. "But I will take you on condition I never hear a word about your children. How you manage is your affair, not mine."

In contrast I am delighted now, as I am involved in training nurses, to hear about all the arrangements hospitals are willing to make to attract nurses with families back into the profession.

Joyce had a very hard time finding a way to raise her children away from their violent father. They lived in a council house, but she could not get the tenancy unless he chose to give it up. Neither could she be considered for a separate tenancy. She was advised many times to stick it out for the sake of the children. She had to rely on her mother and other family members to give her temporary shelter, often causing tension and unhappiness.

In contrast, her daughter's marriage had recently broken down. She still had to deal with the stress and Joyce felt she had been able to be more supportive than if she had also been required to supply the family with basic necessities. Instead the daughter had been able to get a separation and maintenance order and to hold on to the tenancy of her house.

Annie had seen all three of her children go to university and had seen her daughter offered as many opportunities for work as her sons. In addition her daughter had been able to take maternity leave knowing her job was safe. She felt that women were still slower to get promotion because of time out, but this was a far cry from Annie's experience of being told she could not continue to work once she married. We were not sure how much of that practice had been to do with releasing jobs for men and how much was to do with the belief that raising a family was incompatible with teaching.

We all agreed that we had a lot to be grateful for and that our quality of life was a great improvement on that of our mothers and grandmothers. But there seemed to be plenty of evidence around us to show that the world is still biased in favour of men. What we would really like is for women to be allowed and encouraged to be different from men but equal. Our daughters are often fighting for equality and then finding that they have to be like men but better. Perhaps we have to rely on our granddaughters to redress the balance.

PAULETTE BAUCKHAM

Empowerment through talking

In the late 1950s reminiscence was recognized as a positive tool having the potential to make an impact on the quality of life of older people. Before then it was felt that it was just something that "old" people did: the "I remember when" syndrome which was met with raised eyes, a look towards heaven and a muttered "How many times have I heard this before?" Our views changed as we sat and listened to older people recalling memories of their earlier life. We began to realize that they seemed to gain more vivacity and spirit as they remembered.

Until the early 1980s there was no specific name for what they were doing. Then, in 1981, Help the Aged's education department produced a set of slides and tapes called *Recall* which contained sequences of life from 1900 to 1980. They were designed to encourage group discussion among older people in residential, day-care and hospital settings, and they were bought nationwide by many establishments working with such people.

In essence, reminiscing is the act or process of recalling the past — life experiences that are unique to each of us — and recapturing them to relate those episodes in life that have been good, bad, fun, positive and sad. No one has gone through life without experiencing some, if not all, of these emotions. We are all different by virtue of the experiences that have been part of our lives and have shaped us. To converse with someone sounds a simple thing to do, but in fact it is a skill requiring regular exercise in order to be retained. Carers, it is clear, can assist in supporting those who have, through lack of use, lost the skill to talk informally with others. There are many ways — visual, tactile, smell, auditory and so on — of stirring memories.

In the early 1980s I became recreational manager to the residential homes for older people in the London borough of Newham. I was responsible for a team organizing activities supporting the emotional and social needs of older people in residential care. It was clear to me that taking up a permanent place in a residential home was a painful transition for an older person, and that for most it was not from choice but because they recognized they could no longer live on their own without being in some danger — that they could no longer cope.

In many cases, I found, confidence and self-worth could be at very low ebb and, while the level of physical care offered in the homes I was working with was beyond reproach, the emotional and social needs of many individuals were often not being met.

Residents sat in their chairs, staring dispiritedly into space, and they were often depressed since there was little but the next meal to motivate them. When it came to music and movement, art groups, quiz times or outings, it was always the same few people who were involved. I found that negative attitudes were often being internalized by older people, resulting all too often in involuntary disengagement.

But then I saw a video of a working reminiscence group and I could see that older people's spirits were lifted as they were encouraged to speak of their past and the way of life of which they used to be a part. The video excited me and filled me with hope. The scope was boundless — we could encourage older people to talk of their past, not just in passing but as a recognized activity for which time would deliberately be found. I went on a short course and made contact with Mike Bender, then clinical psychologist at Newham. We agreed that reminiscence was something we could offer the physically frail as well as, suitably modified, the sensory impaired and those in various stages of dementia.

Recognizing the worth of reminiscence and the need to bring something more than bingo into older people's lives, the then principal manager at Newham, Mervyn Eastman, gave his full support to establishing reminiscence programmes at fifteen of the borough's residential homes. Initially we were met with distrust and inertia, and in some instances the staff would show the slides more as a picture show than as a means to an end.

We set about promoting group work, working on a basis of six residents and two care staff, guiding and teaching ourselves as went along. Skill and knowledge were necessary, with staff taking account of who should sit next to whom, where to place the shy, quiet or indifferent ones and where those who were talkative or dominant or confused.

We had to learn to deal with anger, pain and sorrow, emotions that surfaced at unpredictable moments. For instance, when an East London group was discussing food as a "waste not want not" subject, it was accepted that stale bread was used for bread pudding and was a regular item in one's diet. This seemed a matter of no real consequence until I noticed that Gladys was sitting in her wheelchair crying silently. I asked if we had upset her, and she said: "Bread pudding was my George's favourite food." I tried to change the subject, but she said: "No, it's OK", and continued to sit there quietly, listening and smiling.

Over a matter of months we were able to define the "art" and were eventually running in-house training courses in group work. A book based on the work we did, called *Group Work with the Elderly*, which I co-wrote with Mike Bender and Andrew Norris, was published by the Winslow Press.

Some of the staff at residential homes felt that reminiscence was an easy option and implied that those engaged in it were opting out of real work. But when an older person has failing eyesight or hearing, and when it is hard to read the newspaper or take in radio or television, their ability to converse, when they have been starved of companionship, can provide nourishment without which they could dry up and become dull and barren.

Interacting with the frail elderly in reminiscence is far from easy, and this is never more true than with the confused who will wring their hands or rock or hum quietly before they tell you something of their lives. Thus Etty, aged eighty-three, would sit, continually muttering "me me me me", until we put on a tape of children playing and she caught the sounds of a skipping rhyme. She stood up, as though she had a rope in her hand, turning and making wide circles as she sang:

> All in together, girls,
> Never mind the weather, girls.
> When I call your birthday,
> Please jump in . . .

and we went on, laughing and without faltering, through all the months of the year.

With others we used tactile material and talked about working for a living. Alf rarely spoke with any meaning until we handed him a metal rivet. This he fondled lovingly for some time and then said: "I built ships, you know." Five minutes later he looked at one of us and said: "Do I know you, dear?"

So is the effort really worth it at the end of the day? The answer has to be: Yes. For a moment you have opened the door and seen inside what makes a person unique. Older people who have seemed to be withdrawn or lacking in confidence, rarely showing any sparkle, change when they are in a reminiscence group. Ellen, who was grumpy for so much of the time, came to life through reminiscence. She smiled as she recaptured her youth, recalling how she had won cups for roller-skating and had been a "wow" with the lads.

Most old people enjoy talking about their past, and discussing their own experiences gives them a feeling of well-being, worth and of being valued. Some, on the other hand, want to share difficult or painful memories. Caroline, aged eighty-nine, quietly told how when she was twelve her "uncle" used to visit her home every week to collect the rent and bath her. She followed this with: "I've never told anyone that before." Staff will quickly find that preconceived views or stereotypical labels applied to older people are often dispelled.

There is now a plethora of reminiscence material available, and reminiscence has become a many-sided tool with various functions, encouraging intergenerational communication and helping young people to understand how people used to live. It is a way of creating a cultural legacy, of establishing a permanent record of the past and how people lived. It can be a way of helping people who may have left their homeland, their history and their culture behind them. Reminiscence can also be fun, even a tonic, and can rejuvenate a group that was rather tired or bored when it started.

But, more than this, it can also promote dialogue between staff and clients and between client and client. It can trigger spontaneous conversation and assist in forming relationships. It can increase a person's self-esteem, help with independence and add to the empowerment of older people. The resulting sense of well-being can be a springboard for greater involvement with other people and in life generally. To be socially involved will not put years on a person's life, but it will put life into their years.

IVOR SMITH-CAMERON

Unfolding faiths

As a result of advances in technology the globe has shrunk, and whoever we are, or wherever we are, we all now inhabit a global village and never more so than in a large metropolitan area. Such a sea change in the way we live has resulted in significant changes in religious attitudes (among both older people and the young) and in community and race relations. Until fairly recently each religion inhabited and flourished in its own particular region: Hinduism in India; Islam in the Middle East; Buddhism in South East Asia and the Far East; and Christianity with its focus in Europe and North America. All this has now changed and changed radically and irreversibly.

In Britain today there are 2 million Muslims — more than the membership of the Methodist, Baptist and United Reformed Churches put together. After Durban, Leicester is now the largest Hindu city outside India. There are more Jews to the square mile in the London Borough of Redbridge than in the state of Israel. Nightingale House in Balham, south London, is the largest

Jewish home for the elderly in Europe. Southall in west London is reckoned to be the capital of the Sikhs outside the Punjab. Every few months new Buddhist monasteries and other centres spring up in the British countryside, peopled mostly by white Buddhist nuns and monks. Today no Londoner lives more than a half-hour journey from a mosque, a Hindu temple, a gurdwara (where Sikhs worship), a synagogue and a vihara (Buddhist centre) as well as a church.

In this new, complex, dynamic and pluralistic situation we need to consider the attitudes that are adopted by the members of these various faith-communities towards older people in their midst. Many have lived in Britain for two, three or four decades and have themselves grown old here. These women and men have undergone many changes in their attitudes to religion, family mores and cultural differences, and above all they have had to confront the gradual ebbing of faith and religious commitment which is one result of secularism.

There was a time when, whether you were a Christian, a Jew, a Hindu, a Muslim, a Buddhist or a Sikh, you lived your faith within a context which was drenched and soaked in religious practices, customs, rites and ceremonies. Your religious beliefs coloured your attitude to life issues, including the treatment of older people, the significance of death and so on. Today, at the dawn of a new millennium, we in Europe confront a civilization which has had the religious dimension filtered out of the very air which we all breathe.

Secularism has not annihilated religion and faith (in fact there is evidence of a growing appreciation of faith today), but in all faith communities it has certainly drastically loosened our links with institutional religion. This has had both advantages and disadvantages.

The following are just a few brief reflections on how faith communities today approach the question of older people in their midst. This is a vitally important subject, deserving of our attention, for it is also complex, unfolding all the time.

In Buddhism there is a very strong emphasis on the performing of *kõyõ*, which means deep filial piety. All Buddhists are encouraged to practise filial piety and perform *kõyõ*. In the strand of Buddhism called Mahayana a great movement has arisen called "the final vehicle" or "the great career", an allusion to the career of what is known as a Bodhisattva, a future Buddha. Buddhists are called upon — especially as they grow older — to attain nirvana (enlightenment), but Mahayana Buddhism emphasizes that it is better to aim to attain nirvana in the distant future and, in the meanwhile, both in one's attitudes towards the elderly and in the attitudes of the elderly, to become as perfect as possible by helping all living beings. Therefore it is seen as a good thing, when growing old, to take the Bodhisattva vow.

Christianity in Britain springs from many roots, but new roots have developed from the sorts of Christianity that are practised in Africa, Asia and the Caribbean. From them has come a very strong emphasis on the extended family; Christians from those parts of the world have a very strong sense of community, and older men and women in the community play a leading role as advisers, senior friends, interpreters of religious traditions, patriarchal and matriarchal models for the rest of the community. Of course the longer these communities have been exposed to secular Western culture the looser their links have become with the community's original spiritual base, often resulting in conflict between generations.

Christian women and men who belong to the ethnic majority in British society have experienced an erosion of their faith. Where in former times the sense of family was strong, in recent years, especially since the Second World War, there has been a shift towards the nuclear family, and community spirit has been replaced by individualism. This has led, some think unfortunately, to a mushrooming of homes for older people. In the best of these institutions individual care is excellently dispensed, but, alas, in the worst of them an atmosphere of hopelessness, loneliness, alienation and of being "cast off" is all too apparent.

Mobility; the break-up of marriages; the loss, for one reason or another, of authority figures; the increase in the number of men and women both working; the liberating effects of feminism; the fact that most women and men now live much longer than they used to (as a priest I very often conduct funerals for people over eighty-five or ninety): all these factors have contributed to what could become the "ghettoization" of old people in Britain. With successive generations now lost to the Christian faith, the strong sense of hope, purpose and meaning that came with the practice of religion is greatly weakened. This will have profound consequences for the future.

Hindu women and men have a concept of life as separated into distinct phases. The final phase, according to Hindu scriptures, is venerated as a stage when the person embarks on a life of penance, prayer and spiritual discipline. This is often referred to as the "life of a *sannayasi*" and it is an honoured life. It is a life of simplicity, a withdrawal from the busy routine of life, given over to works of charity and prayer. Leading Indians like Rabindranath Tagore and Mahatma Gandhi have often been seen as icons of simplicity. Their lives expressed an avowed refusal to be caught up in the rat-race of consumerism which leads to intellectual and cultural voluptuousness. The *sannayasi*'s aspiration to "eat only what he could hold in the palm of his hand" leads to a spiritual growth denied those who are prone to greed. The lives of elderly Hindus often express a concentration on seeking the Divine, and most of them have shrines erected in their homes.

Jewish people have always had a sense of their own identity, and this remains strong even today. While there has been some haemorrhaging of the Jewish community in Britain, there is still a very sharp sense of preserving the Jewishness of their people even among the aged in the community. Though religious observance may not be as strong as Jewish leaders might like, older Jews retain a very strong sense of the cultural and social practices of the faith.

Among Muslims there is a very firm commitment towards older people, strongly reinforced by what is taught in the Holy Qur'an. The Prophet Mohammed (peace be upon him and his family) said: "The honourable person among my followers is he who respects the elders" and "An old person in the house is the same as a prophet is in the community or amongst the nation." (The job of a prophet is to guide his people, act as a role model for the community, admonish wrongdoers and so on.)

In the Shi'ite tradition the Imams have reinforced this teaching. The Sixth Imam, Ja'fer As'sadique, said: "Respect your elders and be kind to your blood relations", and the Fourth Imam, Ali Zainul Abideen, said: "Think of your fellow brothers in faith better than yourself. The elders are better than you because they have had more opportunities to do good and virtuous deeds. As for people younger than yourself — their sins are fewer than yours. People of your age are better because you are aware of your own sins but unaware of their sins."

The Sikh tradition, with its emphasis on community and hospitality, produces among older exponents of the faith women and men who commit themselves to good works and love for their fellow humans. Many devote themselves to serving God in prayer and serving their fellow beings (of whatever faith or none) with food and charity. It is a very pleasing experience to be on the receiving end of a Sikh's unquestioning and non-judgemental hospitality.

These brief reflections on the situation of the older section of our population show that the religious dimension of life, even in a highly secularized society, has not been obliterated. In fact, it persists and has shown a vitality and resilience which cannot be gainsaid.

GILLIAN FORD

Good mourning

Man is made for joy and woe
And when this we rightly know,
Safely through this world we go . . .
— G.K. Chesterton

We find out very quickly, as children, that this world is not a safe place, however much our parents and other adults wish it were and try to make it so. An internationally recognized expert on bereavement is Dr Colin Murray-Parkes, whose interest in the subject was awoken at the age of eight, as he watched the reaction of his family to the death of their dog. I remember a similar event in my own family, when a beloved kitten was run over. The house echoed with his absence — the slightly open door round which his head would have appeared, his toys, his empty basket, no fluffy ears and bright eyes materializing over the edge of the bath. I remember thinking my six-year-old brother was devoid of all sensibility as he played noisily with his friends in this house of mourning. In retrospect, I think we missed out on the ceremony of burying the cat in the garden with attendant obsequies, which would have been so much better than simply his failure to return from the vet's surgery.

But, as I look back on such losses of childhood, I am aware that the intense sadness over the kitten's death contrasts strongly with the emotions I experienced seven years earlier when my cousin (only a year older) died. Then, curiosity was the dominant emotion. I kept asking myself why the grown-ups were always falling silent when children came into the room. What actually happened at funerals? I fell to wondering whether funerals were held after someone had died or before. (So they could join in, I think my reasoning went.)

Children's experiences of death, be it of insects lovingly placed in matchboxes, of foxes or domestic animals on the road, or of grandparents and other family members, is complemented by their experiences of other losses — the stolen bicycle, the doll left behind in the motorway café, the inseparable friend who moves to another town, parental divorce. All these things shape our relationships and prepare us in some measure to cope with the more devastating losses we meet on life's journey. We find ways of moving on — not forgetting the absentee but accepting the loss.

It used to be said that death was the great taboo, but the books, television programmes and newspapers of our own time suggest that this is no longer so. In many parts of the Western world the rituals may be much pared down from those of earlier centuries, but the literature of death is voluminous. What does this suggest about our attitudes to our own deaths — and those near to us?

Forty years ago, medical students were taught that patients would lose all hope if they were told their illness was fatal. This knowledge was shared with their next of kin, but with patients themselves a charade of optimism was maintained. "Well, we'll have to see how it goes." "Oh no, it's not cancer, just a little lump which we can take away." "We'll soon have you up and about." Doctors didn't like lying but thought it was in everybody's best interest that they do so.

Unfortunately the patient was often left bewildered about the lack of straightforward communication. "It seemed so strange that nobody would talk to me," they would muse, while relatives, who did know, found a treacherous divide now yawning between them and the patient — the person they loved. Feelings had to be suppressed and the semblance of normality retained at all costs.

Rattling the cage of this paternalist culture in the 1960s were two remarkable women. The psychiatrist Elizabeth Kübler Ross worked in a Chicago hospital and was initially refused permission by the doctors to talk with dying patients. In the end she succeeded and found all but one of 300 patients delighted to be able to talk about their feelings.

In this country Cicely Saunders, working first as a nurse and then as a social worker, became concerned with every aspect of dying and went on to qualify as a doctor specifically to remedy the neglect she had seen. She soon came to believe that the practice of well-meaning deception destroyed trust between patients and their families and friends and between patients and the professionals caring for them. Moreover it denied people the opportunity to make some sense of the time remaining to them, of doing the last things they wanted to do, such as drawing up a will or trying to say "I'm sorry" or "I love you".

Laurens Van der Post, in *A Story like the Wind*, wrote:

No imagination has yet been great enough to invent improvements to the truth. Truth, however terrible, carries within itself its own strange comfort for the misery it is so often compelled to inflict on behalf of life. Sooner or later it is not pretence but the truth which gives back with both hands what it has taken away with one. Indeed, unaided and alone, it will pick up the fragments of the reality it has shattered and piece them together in the shape of more immediate meaning than the one in which they had previously been contained.

The caring professions did not accept the validity of all this overnight. The direction of modern medicine still leans towards treatment-based care and health, and death challenges professional competence. Nevertheless nurses soon welcomed the improved relationships with patients which became possible once deception was banished. Doctors came to realize that discussion of a patient's prognosis, however grave, was part of the doctor-patient relationship and that caring for dying patients requires just as much involvement, research and expertise as traditional clinical practice.

Most people say that it is not death itself that they fear but the process of dying. And with reason. Progressive weakness, the small day-by-day physical retreats leading inexorably to a loss of control and dignity and the overwhelming sensations of uselessness and dependency are all part of late-stage disease, and there are no easy prescriptions and slick remedies for them. But, again, attitudes and expertise have changed enormously since my days as a medical student and junior doctor.

I arrived at St Thomas' Hospital in 1956 only knowing a few people. One was Cicely Saunders with whom, a year or two later, I shared a flat. Her mission to improve the care of the dying was, even then, gathering momentum and it was a huge privilege to be so closely associated with the thinking, planning, prayer, research, grant applications and networking of those early stages. Even as a pre-registration house officer I was encouraged to put into practice some of her innovative precepts about pain and symptom control — the regular giving of effective pain relief being at that time almost unheard of.

The establishment of St Christopher's Hospice in south London in 1967 was a natural way to show how much could be done for patients with cancer. Instead of treating the very ill with a kind of benign neglect, we discovered that so much could be improved by listening and noting in detail what the problems were, by dealing with distressing symptoms, by recognizing that mental and spiritual pain might be just as hard to bear as nausea and vomiting, by concentrating on the quality of the life that is left.

Thirty years and more on from there, we see how this one small development emerged in the context of a broader trend towards social open-mindedness. The themes are familiar — women's right to control their own bodies, greater freedom of speech between the sexes and generations, new ideas about learning so well exemplified by the Open University, the break-up of rigid professional castes and the impact on our own society of the beliefs and attitudes of other cultures. Little wonder that the development of the hospices and palliative care teams was so warmly welcomed and spontaneously supported in communities right across this country — and, indeed, throughout the world.

Cicely Saunders has often been urged to "clone" St Christopher's in other places. But she has had the wisdom to suggest that her model was not one set in tablets of stone and that others would see how best to address the needs of their own communities. This was surely the mark of a great innovator rather than an ideology-bound reformer. Nevertheless one cannot fail to be impressed by the universality of the principles and the similarities of approaches elsewhere, whether in Australia or Zimbabwe, Iceland or Ireland.

The increasing number of hospice developments, of professions with special concern for dying people, cancer charities and palliative care services, both voluntary and NHS, led to the creation in the UK of a National Council which represents these bodies in negotiations with the government and other national institutions. Even more important than its representative and awareness-raising role has been the council's activity in encouraging and producing seminal documents aimed at improving the care of people with late-stage disease, wherever they may be and whatever the cause of their illness.

Not all the demons of dying have been conquered. Half a century ago people looked to their families for emotional and practical support; the routines, and the attitudes and faith that lay behind them, were generally known and accepted. In short, the family was the focus of the passage through life — and the leaving of it. Today families are generally smaller and more fragmented and far from unified in their outlooks and their beliefs. It is this change which makes such a contrast between then and now. Today there are formal professional networks of support, and while they may help both the dying and the bereaved they lack the warmth and staying power which, in earlier generations, sustained people through all the crises of life. The multi-professional team, however caring, cannot make up for the loss of control and independence experienced as strength ebbs away. The crippling inability to be useful to anybody, to accept that one cannot always be the good Samaritan, may bring to the fore feelings of frustration and anger and a desire to bring matters to a head at a time and in a way of one's own choosing.

Voluntary euthanasia is increasingly a matter of public debate. From time to time the law of this land, which forbids anybody — whether doctor, caring friend or spouse — from actively taking steps to end life, is tested. Sometimes this is in the context of ending treatment or procedures that are only prolonging life — or the semblance of it. Artificial feeding and hydration are regarded as treatments which can be withdrawn, though a court order may be necessary to do so. Many people now endeavour to avoid futile prolongation of their own lives — or, more accurately, their own dying — by drawing up advance directives. While these are not legally enforceable, they are useful indicators of their wishes in the matter.

A strong case can be made by ideologues who are happy to make free with other people's lives to sustain a principle. But, before legally assisted death can be looked at as a possibility, there is much to consider that is not mere debate. Against calculated resource arguments in its favour stand moral arguments of great power which are not easily measured or turned into social policy. My first consideration is the pressure that would begin to operate against frail old people, who would actually prefer to depart in their own, or God's, good time.

More important than legislation for death, and the eerie shadow that it would cast, is that greater effort should be made to ensure that life continues to be liveable at whatever age or stage. I have a strong feeling, too, that very old people and the dying have things to teach us which could be missed in a preoccupation with premature departure. An old friend of my husband phoned him to announce that he had only a few days to live. We hurried to the hospital where his bed was surrounded with papers, photographs and pots of tea, while he himself was full of ideas about his planned memorial meeting. As he ran over so many remembered events and relationships, he managed, in fact, to review his own life and what he held most important in it — all with great humour and charm — and in so doing delighted, not saddened, the company of his wife, sister and his friends.

A sudden and unexpected death is something many of us wish for ourselves. We think it would be uncomplicated, with none of that difficult business of dying and seeing people grieving for us. But such a death does not include the opportunity to tackle some of the untidiness of departure and to share with those most dear to us the pain of parting.

For some of us it is not death and dying which are the hard things but being left behind. Even if the burden of depression is bearable, the practicalities of life may defeat us. Some spouses have never paid bills or filled the car's petrol tank, while for others cooking and the washing machine, or even getting children ready for school, are arcane mysteries known only by the missing halves. These are, of course, the relatively unimportant things, and a younger generation is coming along with shared, rather than defined roles, in work and partnership. Whatever the age group, however, grief, guilt and loneliness make their unwelcome presence felt, tarnishing the brightest day with thoughts beginning "If only . . ." or "I wish . . ." And then there is fear. Fear that we will never again know contentment or peace — or, paradoxically, that we will forget the one who has died and that this is tantamount to disloyalty or even betrayal.

The bound-to-happen bereavements of older people — spouses, siblings, friends of the same age — may be more threatening, even if less of a shock, than those of younger people, for a variety of reasons. No longer is there the daily round of work to distract; the family circle is smaller; new relationships are far less likely to happen (even if wanted, even if they can be sustained). There are also problems such as poor health or failing sight, hearing or mobility, which make another loss even more difficult to bear. Death comes in so many ways and guises that it demands a whole range of responses from us, who are often unprepared, and always calls forth new thoughts and new emotional efforts.

I think particularly of the death of a son or a daughter in their prime or of a grandchild. This is really the most dreadful of tragedies. We long to be able to take their place as we have already lived our lives. The surrogate loss we suffer for them, the hopes of life unfulfilled, the future not seen, somehow forges a painful but tender link across the generations and reminds us again that man is, indeed, made for "joy and woe". Personally, as I face these things, I hope for grace, to be able to accept the care I may need from others, for there to be no unfinished business or unresolved anger and to be able to remember the bright days, and the good things that life has brought, but not to mourn them.

MANAGING — OR COPING

Barbara Castle

Dave Goodman

Michael Dunne

Angela Willans

Gordon Macpherson

BARBARA CASTLE

Pensions and politics

Those of us who most want to help everyone enjoy their later years to the full are in danger of defeating our own ends. By constantly harping on the word "age" — Help the Aged, Age Concern, the campaign against ageism — we play into the hands of our enemies. Names are important. They affect attitude, and it is attitudes that dictate policy.

When I was first elected to the European Parliament in 1979, I was invited to join its Committee on Ageing. The very words put years on me and I refused, saying that the only committee in which I might be interested would be a committee on keeping young. I had just been voted a member of the first directly elected European Parliament, and the local parties which had selected me felt my experience was needed to guide them through this strange new political world.

One delegate had indeed pointed out that I was sixty-nine. To this I retorted that Jim Callaghan, who was only two years younger than I was, had just been selected by the Labour Party to follow Harold

Wilson as Prime Minister. My reminder did the trick.

I am not suggesting that we older 'uns should hang on to office or power indefinitely, blocking the way for the younger ones. On the contrary, I had refused to fight the 1979 election to the House of Commons, despite pleas from my Blackburn comrades that I should do so, because I wanted to make way for the younger ones who would be a our future ministers. All I am urging is that each situation should be judged on its merits and that candidates should not be ruled out by some arbitrary drawing of a line.

Lord Denning, who died recently at the age of a hundred after many years of service to British justice, was eighty-three years old when he retired as Master of the Rolls. He has been acclaimed as the greatest judge of the century and, to the end, he was dispensing the wisdom he had acquired over many years. He was the embodiment of Tennyson's lyric from "The Princess":

Oh, I feel the crescent promise of my spirit
   hath not set.
Ancient founts of inspiration well within my
   fancy yet . . .

But how do we reconcile these two demands — not to stand in the way of the legitimate ambitions of the young while not allowing the hungry generations to tread us down?

It is easy for you to talk, I can hear readers say. Some professions, like politics, have no statutory retirement age: *vide* Sir Edward Heath, born in 1916 and still hanging on in his eighties to the pinnacle of his parliamentary career as Father of the House of Commons.

The self-employed can hang on until they drop. The wealthy can pick and choose. But most of us have to retire when the rules of our pension say that we must. Some of us in this harsh competitive world are not even allowed to go on working to retirement age. Millions of the older generation face a daily struggle to survive.

So what can be done? The answer, I believe, lies in a revolutionary change in attitudes. We must all, both young and old, be taught to look on life as a gradually unfolding drama in which the different stages overlap, just as the seasons do, and in which each season, even winter, has its beauty and its role.

My revolution would start with pensions. In my bulging post-bag I have been particularly struck by a letter I received not long ago from a woman begging me to start a campaign against the use of the word "pensioner". I knew what she meant. Over the years it has acquired patronizing, almost pitying overtones. Once you have reached a certain point in your life you are "pensioned off" with the suggestion that you have now become a burden on society. You no longer have an economic function. If you are well off and healthy, life can still be full. If not, you have to be bailed out of an inadequate income by the charity of means-tested benefits.

So let us begin by finding a new name which recognizes that at sixty or sixty-five you may still have half your life to live at a time when medical science is keeping us healthier longer. If the experts are right, life expectancy in the next century will have extended to 130 years for many of us. Few of us would want to be "pensioned off" all that time.

We must put on our thinking caps for a new concept to go with a new name. What about, for instance, getting people to insure for a "halfway house income", enough to live on for those who can no longer work or do not wish to but on which the more active of us could build a second and perhaps more modest job? For the luckier among us this is already commonplace.

There are certain practical implications in what I propose. A "halfway house income" could possibly involve retirement from one's main career, making room for younger aspirants. By definition, it could not be means-tested since that would make the second income meaningless and would defeat the government's aim of switching the emphasis from welfare to work.

But is my idea practical? Economics rules all our lives, and the sums must add up. I see no difficulty in financing the first-stage income under my policy, as some of us have been demonstrating statistically in pamphlets and articles. I would refer, for instance, to the publication *Fair Shares for Pensions* co-authored by myself and Peter Townsend and available from Security in Retirement for Everyone, 27–29 Amwell Street, London EC1R 3UN, at £5 or £1.50 unwaged.

What worries me most about this government's pensions proposals is that they are out of date. They are a throwback to the Malthusian-type concept that the wealth of a nation is limited, that priority must be given to the wealth creators and that compassion for the rest must involve the poorest pensioner being means-tested. Dividing society between the weakest of us and those who are strong enough to pay their way is the very approach which has led political parties to compete on the grounds that they have kept down the cost of the "deserving poor". But the revolutionary solution that the 1945 Labour government adopted from Beveridge was based on his belief that poverty and degradation were not acts of God and that the five giant evils — Disease, Ignorance, Squalor, Idleness and Want — could be conquered by the proper organization of society's resources.

Beveridge was no starry-eyed romantic but a tough-minded Liberal who had no use for the inequalities and inefficiencies of the hand-out society. Instead, he argued that everyone in work should be compelled by law to contribute when at work to a national insurance scheme which would provide them with a basic security from the cradle to the grave. He realized that the insurance scheme must be underpinned by nationally organized health

101

care and a policy to defeat unemployment in years of depression. He also realized that it was no good lecturing people about the duty to work if there was no work for them to do.

Since his day our social and economic life has become much more sophisticated, and with the triumph of free-market economics state insurance has become the poor relation. Even under the Labour government of the 1960s the basic pension was allowed to dwindle to the point at which it had to be supplemented by means-tested benefits. The Labour government of 1974 made a determined effort to reverse this trend. Its first step was to put backbone into the state pension by obliging governments by law to uprate it annually and to keep it in line with rising national prosperity through the earnings link.

By the 1970s the more fortunate white-collar workers had been able to negotiate with their employers, whether government or private, new forms of earnings-related superannuation or occupational pension schemes. In 1974 Labour extended this privilege to all those who were not included in this magic circle by introducing a second-tier state earnings-related pension, SERPS. This, too, was compulsory, but contributors were free to contract out into an occupational pension scheme which guaranteed them the same security. The main aim was to give everyone the right to an updated basic security within income limits while giving them the freedom to build on this by additional private insurance, if they so wished and could afford it.

The pensions insurance companies applauded this because they have never pretended that they could cater for those who are on low or modest incomes. They were glad that the state would take over the responsibility for providing for those who did not have the resources to gamble on the market as private insurance does.

The tragedy is that New Labour has accepted Margaret Thatcher's mutilation of those state insurance schemes. The basic pension is to continue to shrink by perpetuating her rejection of the earnings link. SERPS is to be phased out and replaced eventually by a "stakeholder pension" the size of which will depend on the state of the stock markets. It will be underpinned by a means-tested safety net for the "poorest" pensioners.

Society is to continue to be divided between rich and poor from the cradle to the grave. The stigma of age is to remain linked with the stigma of dependency. In early 1999 a government minister admitted in reply to a parliamentary question that on the basis of present policies approximately 3.5 million pensioners (one in three) could still be dependent on a minimum income guarantee in the year 2050, in other words on means-tested support. Such a pension policy is an uneasy bedfellow of the NHS whose ethic is based on the belief that everyone should contribute when they are fit and enjoy the support of society when they are ill. We can all imagine what would happen to our national health care if it were to be means-tested and people were to be induced to pin their hopes on private health insurance, which most of them could not afford in any case.

So why should not the same arguments apply to the third stage of our lives? What most of us need is three tiers of provision. The first is the basic security of an adequate contributory guaranteed halfway-house income which is ours by right and uprated annually in line with earnings. Under a "pay as you go" scheme this will mean adjustments in contributions from time to time. Any increase should, of course, be shared with the employer as it is in any good superannuation scheme.

The cost to state insurers could also be reduced if, for example, their contributions to state pensions were given the same tax relief as contributors to personal pensions enjoy (this concession is costing the Treasury £2.6 billion in the current year, with tax relief on contributions to occupational pension schemes costing another £8.5 billion on top). Instead, the government seems bent on relieving the employers of their share of the contributory scheme and shifting the cost of the associated means-tested safety net to the taxpayer.

On this firm foundation, we could then build our second tier: a job adapted to our capabilities and our desires. It must be sunk deep into the national consciousness that the over-sixties have a vital economic contribution to make to our society.

Some may prefer to make that contribution voluntarily. Others may prefer — or need — a paid job. It is not a question of "creating" jobs since we all know there are thousands of them, in which experience and maturity are invaluable, crying out to be done.

The government has made a good start with its campaign to convince employers that it is short-sighted folly to turn their backs on the talents of the over-fifties, but it is time to start campaigning for the over-sixties too. Many of the jobs I have in mind will be in the public services, which have a vital role to play in the quality of our national life. Here it is a question of loosening the Treasury's restrictions on public expenditure. But there is plenty of scope as well in the private field, and retailers, for example, are beginning to appreciate the commercial value of older workers in helping and advising customers. Some DIY firms and others are already making a selling point of employing over-sixties who really know what the customer is talking about! It is also the government's job to stimulate economic growth so that our economy can make use of all those who want to work.

Of course, there will come a time in all our lives when we can no longer work. In a civilized society this stage must be handled with the utmost sensitivity. This means helping us to retain our identity for as long as possible. Local services must be expanded to enable us to stay as long as possible in our own homes, and we must be spared the cruelty of having to sell all but a few thousand pounds of our assets to pay for residential care.

The Royal Commission on Long Term Care set up by the government under the chairmanship of Professor Sir Stewart Sutherland has issued a complex and challenging report. Most of us can agree with some of its recommendations for funding this final stage of our lives, if not all of them. I for one heartily endorse the report's statement that "private insurance will not deliver what is required at an acceptable cost, nor does the industry want to provide that degree of coverage".

I would like to see state insurance carry some of the burden of funding long-term care. Others would not agree with me — not even, I gather, the report's authors. But what is clear from this valuable definition of the problem is that we need to start an open debate and discussion without delay. We cannot continue any longer with the present hotch-potch provision of long-term care or lack of it. Working out an alternative is one of the most important tasks facing our society.

DAVE GOODMAN

Tightening the belt

When you become a pensioner, how you budget depends on the place you occupy among Britain's well over 10 million senior citizens. Their income range is extremely wide, including 100,000 (just 1 per cent) who pay top-rate tax. Among them will be quite a few millionaires and perhaps the odd billionaire. They are not the subject of this essay.

At the bottom end of the income range there are around a million (nearly 10 per cent) who are eligible for but do not claim income support (also called Minimum Income Guarantee or MIG). Clearly this is the group of the pensioner population with the greatest need, and theirs is truly a case of budgeting on a pittance.

They know all about "hard choices" such as trying to keep one room warm enough to live during the winter months while maintaining a diet that is adequate. Entertainment and relaxation are mostly provided by television, the licence fee — now over £100 — paid through the weekly purchase of stamps. The cost of transport, even with a bus pass, reduces mobility to a minimum. Holidays are not even thought about, and as pricey durable goods such as cookers and washing machines break down or wear out replacing them with new ones is not an option. The lucky ones may get something passed on from a relative who is acquiring a new model. The government's Social Exclusion Unit has yet to recognize properly this "missing million" that subsist below the level of income support (and the additional benefits that go with it), but they are a major group of Britain's socially excluded.

Somewhat better placed are the 1.5 million who do receive income support plus housing benefit, council tax rebate and other benefits. Their Minimum Income Guarantee is now put at £78. To appreciate the complexities of budgeting on this sort of income you have realize that according to all recent research the amount needed to provide a "modest but adequate" income for a single pensioner is around £150 a week, nearly double the amount guaranteed by the government.

Life on £78 a week is about social exclusion. It is in fact the Poverty Income Guarantee (PIG). Items of expenditure which so many take for granted, such as eating out, buying new clothes or taking holidays at home or abroad, are not accessible to this group. Even buying a daily newspaper can be ruled out by the exigencies of making ends meet on less than £80 a week. Appearances are kept up through occasional purchases of clothes from charity shops. A major headache for this group, and the million mentioned earlier, totalling together some 2.5 million people, is their inability to cope with essential home maintenance and repairs.

Moving on to the 8 million pensioners who do not receive income support we find three main groups. At the top end are those with good vocational pensions and income from savings and investment. Budgeting for them is no great hardship. Whole house heating is not a problem, they can afford to eat out, buy new clothes, maintain their properties, take holidays and, subject to health, generally enjoy a quality of life equivalent to that of their pre-retirement days. These are former business people or members of a range of professions or careers in public service. Some of them belong to branches of Probus (Professional/Business), an offshoot of the Rotary Club for its retired members.

At the bottom end of this group there is a marked contrast. Here we find those, and there are many, who fail to qualify for income support by a small margin owing to having some income additional to the basic pension, either from a works pension or from savings. They would be better off without that extra income because then they could then receive much more in income support and additional benefits. This group, too, swells the numbers of those budgeting on a pittance. Though the government claims to be targeting "the poorest pensioners", in practice that means only those on income support. It fails to recognize the existence of those just over the income support threshold who, by any definition, should be included among "the poorest pensioners".

The failure of the government until now to restore the link between the basic pension and earnings, while increasing income support/MIG by more than inflation and linking it to earnings, would have the effect of making many more pensioners eligible for means-tested income support, though if they have savings above £8,000 these will have to be depleted first. It should be noted that this policy runs counter to Labour's policy in opposition, which condemned the ending of the earnings link as a betrayal by the Tories of present and future pensioners. It is also out of line with Labour's election manifesto pledges. These said that the basic pension would be maintained as a foundation of pension provision. In fact it is being allowed to wither on the vine, shrinking annually in value relative to earnings.

The Labour manifesto also pledged that all pensioners should share fairly in rising national prosperity. To deliver that pledge an effective mechanism is essential to ensure that as living standards rise pensioners are not left behind.

The present government likes to boast about its record of delivering its commitments, with hardly an exception. So it is strange that it should have a blind spot for the generation to whom it pays lip-service every year when Remembrance Day comes round. Yet this is the generation among the pensioner population without whose efforts and sacrifices at home and overseas there would have been no future for the generations that followed. What kind of nation and government is it that leaves them to budget on a pittance?

The poverty entailed in budgeting on a pittance is not immediately obvious. It is no coincidence that the market for second-hand clothes is big enough to sustain a vast number of charity shops. While some people who normally buy new clothes occasionally buy something from a charity shop, for millions of senior citizens there is no choice. Their second-hand purchases enable them to look presentable, and the reality of their situation is disguised from public view. Indeed the hardships and suffering so prevalent in the Older Nation are largely borne silently and without complaint, except for those active in campaigning organizations.

Jack Jones is fond of quoting from Nye Bevan that "silent pain evokes no response". I should add that the ability to keep up appearances is, for many pensioners, assisted by thoughtful contributions from members of their families. The most up-to-date and stylish items in my wardrobe are mainly Christmas and birthday presents, from my daughter and late wife in particular. My local paper runs a feature called Street Style, which photographs, with comments, a cross-section of the local populace. When I was chosen as the week's model the comment mentioned that the shirt, tie and (trendy red) braces I was wearing were all presents from my daughter.

The North Staffordshire Pensioners Convention has carried out research, led by academics from Staffordshire University and funded by Charity Projects (Comic Relief), into pensioner budgeting. Its published report, *Life on the Margins*, focused on hidden poverty, and its findings are reflected in this essay. They show that uprating pensions in line with the Retail Price Index does not maintain the purchasing power of the pension. The report concluded that "over time the state pension has fallen behind the real cost of living for pensioners". That can best be illustrated by these extracts from case studies in the report:

> Mr and Mrs A live in a large terrace house near the centre of Stoke. They are aged between 75 and 79 and appear to be coping reasonably well on an income of £99 a week [this was in 1993]. They worried a lot about house maintenance. The house is old and the jobs that need doing are quite big ones. They keep one room heated during winter months and Mr A wears a hat all the time. They do not appear to have any help from members of the family and say they live on a pension by denying themselves. They buy one newspaper a week for the TV programmes. They do not have a social life. They have cut right back on present giving, but feel bad when they receive presents. They need extra money

for clothes (particularly underwear); to decorate the house; keep it warmer and ease their worries about bills.

Mrs B is a widow in her late 60s, living with her son in a rented council house. She receives a single person's pension plus Income Support, out of which she pays £24 weekly rent (in 1993) with two rent-free weeks a year. She wears extra clothing to keep warm in winter. Her son helps with the fuel bills, her children bought her new spectacles for Christmas and she feels she needs new dentures but is put off by the likely cost. She buys clothes from Oxfam or makes her own and would like to replace her coat which was bought more than 20 years ago for her mother's funeral. She pays for her phone and TV with stamps. She keeps in touch by phone with her sister in Wales whom she visited last year thanks to a £20 gift from her son. She was hoping to go again but "would have to go round with the hat first".

Mrs C is quietly spoken, in the 65–69 age bracket. She is worried about bills — food, fuel, housing and so on. Though she is in the lower income group she says she is satisfied with life in general, though she recognizes that without help from her family things would be very different. They buy her presents of "decent clothes", including skirts and coats, at birthdays and at Christmas, and pass on things such as jumpers and cardigans. She has had a microwave and a washing machine from them. This help from family seems to be the difference between poverty and just managing a modest standard of living.

Recently a pensioner wrote to me saying: "It seems to be impossible to make politicians understand what it means to live on a basic pension." He suggested this novel way of getting the message across: "A pensioner on £3,500 a year, if he spends 60p on a bag of tea, 49p on a loaf of bread, 36p on a pint of milk, 99p on a 500-gram tub of Flora, 45p on a tin of soup and £1.05p on a box of cereal, that is a total of £3.94, which represents roughly 17 per cent of his weekly income. If you apply this principle as a proportion of income to an MP on £30,000 a year he or she would be paying £5.10 for a bag of sugar, £4.17 for a loaf of bread, £3.06 for a pint of milk, £8.42 for a tub of Flora, £3.83 for a tin of soup and the box of cereal would be £8.93."

Finally, the issue of budgeting has to be understood in the context that the poverty of most of the Older Nation exists in the midst of plenty — Britain is in the top half-dozen of the world's richest countries. Writing in 1919, J. Bruce Glasier, a close colleague of Keir Hardie, said: "The great wrong of existing social conditions does not lie in the mere circumstance that many are poor while few are rich

. . . but in the denial of brotherhood which these conditions imply. Were all poor alike, the poverty might not only be quite endurable, but great fellowship and happiness might be possible with it." Eleven years earlier David Lloyd George said: "How we treat our old people is a test of our national quality. A nation that lacks gratitude to those who have honestly worked for her in the past whilst they had the strength to do so does not deserve a future, for she has lost her sense of justice and her instinct of mercy."

Is it not long past the time when the nation should no longer be shamed by the presence of so many millions of its citizens, who happen to be senior citizens, who to survive are compelled to budget on a pittance?

MICHAEL DUNNE

Getting and spending

Many older people live alone and depend on an income that is paid weekly. Hence their day-to-day shopping has to consist of small packs of food and cleaning materials which almost always cost more, as a proportion, than a larger quantity. In addition, many older people cannot get to supermarkets and have to rely on corner shops where prices are generally higher. So, for everyday shopping, the poor are penalized by having to pay more. Likewise, the closure of village shops means that travelling costs have to be added to rural shopping bills.

It was not surprising when in 1975 the National Consumer Council's very first report, entitled *For Richer For Poorer*, came to the conclusion that "the poor pay more". How much, I wonder, have things changed in the past quarter-century?

After several years as a researcher on the magazine *Which?* during its early years, I had begun to realize that there should be more to "consumer" research than "value for money" and "best buys". I use the word "consumer" in quotes advisedly. In the developed world the consumer movement, with its concentration on informed choice, has tended (perhaps subconsciously) to breed the concept of the well-nigh limitless acquisition of personal possessions without thought of those for whom choice is often impossible or what the consequences of those choices may be.

As early as 1960 Raymond Williams was contrasting the concepts "consumer" and "user": "It is as consumers that the great majority of people are seen. We are the market which the system of industrial production has organized . . . We have to work to change the poor society of affluent consumers into a rich society of educated users." More explicitly, in his book *The Long Revolution*, published in 1961, he wrote: "If we were not consumers but users, we might look at society very differently. For the concept of use involves general human judgements — we need to know how to use things and what we are using them for, and also the effects of particular uses on our general life — whereas consumption, with its hand-to-mouth patterns, tends to cancel these questions, replacing them with the stimulated and controlled absorption of the products of an external and autonomous system."

So it can be argued that we use information to gain access to health care; to say we "consume" either information or the NHS itself would be ludicrous. For older people the problem of making effective use of services assumes greater importance.

117

Their concerns are with access to welfare benefits, social services, pensions, public transport, health care, appropriate housing and so on.

At the Consumers' Association's sister organization, the Research Institute for Consumer Affairs, I found the aims were to conduct research to determine whether goods and services on offer at the time — commercial, professional and public — were in fact "adequate" to the wants and needs that they claimed to meet. The emphasis was on people's access to and use of goods and services, particularly the needs of older and disabled people.

Equality of access is all-embracing, taking account of people's needs and wants at varying income levels. It also links in with the concept of people, and particularly older people, as users of services. They need equality of access to the ballot box, good housing, health care, transport, fuel, representation in disputes, leisure activities and the means to provide themselves with a reasonable income and provision when no longer able to work. Many older people also need access to worthwhile voluntary activity in retirement, not only because it is much appreciated but to help maintain their self-esteem.

But there are other areas of use and access which apply specifically to older people and their needs. One, in which I have been involved as a researcher relates to fuel and the problem of fuel poverty. This centres on the inability of large numbers of older people to keep warm in winter. Of course, not all older people have low incomes or live in poor housing. But two-thirds of pensioners have incomes so low that they pay no income tax, and half of these live at or below the poverty line. Around 40,000 more people (mainly older people) die from cold-related illnesses in the three winter months than in the summer, a figure that shows no sign of diminishing. Many older people live in the poorest and most difficult-to-heat housing. In the supposedly affluent London Borough of Richmond upon Thames, 38 per cent of pensioners have no central heating, 2,000 live in "unfit" properties and another 1,000 are in homes in substantial disrepair.

Yet such things have been known and documented for thirty years or more. In 1969 the government issued a mandatory standard which specified that housing specially provided for older people should have a heating installation capable of maintaining a temperature of 21°C (71°F) throughout the living areas.

Despite extensive research, lobbying and some remedial action such as insulating and draught-proofing grants, far too many older people do not have access to a warm home. They have to pay more for their fuel (having, for instance, no access to direct debit discounts) with less money to do so and they live in homes which are harder to heat. While any upgrading of the annual winter fuel grant to pensioners is welcome, this will only provide warmer homes at the expense of extra fuel consumption. Improvements to poor housing would provide both more warmth and energy savings.

The importance of equal access to information, covering a range of services, benefits, concessions and other facilities, should be axiomatic. There is an ever-growing supply of leaflets, fact sheets and advice services. Yet studies have shown that for many older people, particularly the immobile, the very old and those living in the country, the information they need is not getting through to them, something that is true for many even when they have frequent contact with family, GPs, district nurses or social workers.

Since the family is the most frequent, if not the most reliable, source of information for many older people, it is important that the younger generation is also well informed about what services are available for older people. There are many possible channels for the periodic issue of information such as Child Benefit payment books, via children at school and at health clinics. Home helps, district nurses and day centre staff need to be better equipped with a knowledge of what benefits and services are available and the agencies that can give detailed advice.

People with a particular need are likely to use information if it is presented at the point in time at which it applies — such as details of home helps and aids to daily living when they are about to be discharged from hospital; details of housing benefit and council tax with the bill from the council; about spectacle vouchers when having their eyes tested; cash for fares to hospital with out-patient appointment letters. Many elderly people do not read much, but they do listen to the radio. This is an under-used source of information on benefits and services which could be incorporated in stories, soap operas and even popular songs.

One older person in every three has no savings, while the savings of another one in three brought in less than £8 a week (in 1994). Many are therefore without the resources to pay for more major household items and have to resort to hire purchase with interest rates up to 25 per cent and then only if they have what is euphemistically called "status". The alternative is door-to-door moneylenders charging even higher rates. In general, older people who are also poor lack equal access to good financial services.

As already mentioned, those without access to a bank account have to pay some 15 per cent more for their gas than those who have access to direct debits. Older people are likely to use the more expensive forms of heating. An old radiant gas fire uses a third as much again in gas as modern central heating for the same amount of heat. Open coal fires are even more wasteful and hence more expensive.

Even when it come to means-tested benefits, those elderly who have saved a few thousand pounds are cheated out of what they have. The amount of income they are assumed to have from savings before benefits are calculated is ludicrously high. Someone with savings of £8,000 is treated as getting a return of 13 per cent.

The catalogue of areas in which there is insufficient equality of access for older people is limitless. They need access to information in plain English — when they speak English — not in gobbledegook; access to banks and financial services, not moneylenders; access to good local shops, not out-of-town hypermarkets; physical access to low-level buses. The trend towards super-hospitals, super-libraries and so on needs careful watching if access for older people is not to be restricted. They also need access to friendly support and help through voluntary good neighbour schemes. And, of course, they need access to an adequate income.

ANGELA WILLANS

Love and lovability

The biggest lesson I've learned from life is that every one of us, whether we know it or not, is on a lifetime search for love and self-esteem and that, in generation after generation but much more so in the past forty years, men and women have blindly sought to fulfil these needs through sex.

Now I reckon that it takes someone of the third age to recognize at last that sex for its own sake rarely leads to love or self-esteem. It doesn't boost your ego. It doesn't fulfil any real emotional needs. It's never the answer to self-doubt. If it does anything at all about loneliness, it usually adds to it. In short, sex can be glorious, life-affirming and fun, but it's primarily a biological imperative, riddled with risks to health and self-image and always a runner-up to the desire to be loved and thought well of.

The reason we have this illusion that sex is the precursor to the prime ingredient of love is an entirely logical one. Where else, except in a sexual relationship, can adults hope to find the tactile warmth and loving attention that they either enjoyed or failed to find in childhood? But the cruel result of dependence on sexual activity as the route to love and respect is that it gets you neither. Instead, what you get is other immature or neurotic people with their needs for obsessional attachments and ego-enhancing sex. Love and self-respect are what you're more likely to get when you're enough of a confident, self-loving person not to desperately need more of the same, nor to look for someone else to supply it — though a top-up never comes amiss. In other words, wanting love very badly indeed means that you don't have enough love in you to give to anyone else — so you crave love but are incapable of loving. This can only be a bad start to a good relationship with yourself or with others.

What we need most from each other throughout our lives is warmth, mutual respect, emotional support, caring and sharing. Homer summed it up in the *Odyssey*: "For there is nothing more potent or better than this; when a man and woman, sharing the same ideas about life, keep house together. It is a thing which causes pain to their enemies and pleasure to their friends. But only they themselves know what it really means." Nothing about sex, one notes, though we can surely include sexual harmony in the concept of "sharing the same ideas about life".

The tragedy of contemporary marriage break-ups, however, is that we put so much emphasis on the Western idea of romantic love and sexual attraction as motives for marriage that when the sex and the heady feeling of being "in love" cool, so does the chance of real loving and the hope of companionship. Unless help is at hand, it may mean the end of the relationship before the couple can turn their perceived loss of "the magic" into real loving which, in its turn, is better than magic.

However, that takes time — which is good news for the over-sixties because by our age we just might have garnered the opportunities, the wisdom and the right partner to have it all and share it. One thing is certain: nobody's love life, let alone their sex life, with a long-time partner or a new one is likely to reach the stars after the age of sixty, unless he or she has already been pretty close to the heavens a few times. In essence, life at sixty plus is probably as good as it gets, as far as relationships go. But that can certainly be very good indeed.

One of the many "put-downs" for love in favour of sex is the age-old taboo on tenderness and the new doubts about romance. These force men and women to pretend that they don't really want respect and consideration — only the sex bit — with the result that they may defensively mock each other's attempts to show any sensitivity or gentler feelings.

Thus the sexual scenario hots up into a competition for who can show the most lust and the least love. And it's no surprise that one of life's saddest ironies rumbles on — the fact that, deep down, women still go on hoping for love on their terms and men continue to give it on theirs — Mars and Venus indeed. But recognizing this without resentment, as many older people do, is halfway to accepting and rejoicing in the difference.

Fortunately, these changes in attitudes can almost be ignored by those over-sixties who are still in a happy partnership. As Homer said, only they themselves know what it really means and, of course, only they themselves need to know. But what of the thousands of people moving into old age on their own? The figures are quite startling. Fifty per cent of the UK population over the age of seventy-five live in single households. Of the men and women between sixty-five and seventy-four, 39 per cent live alone. In both age groups women outnumber men — in the older age group by almost double. This is an increasing change in the way we live, and it raises the question of whether there's a lot more loneliness about than there used to be.

In the 1960s, when I started as an agony aunt, loneliness in all its forms was the Number One problem in the thousands of letters that came to me every week. There's no reason now to suppose that the problem of loneliness is getting any smaller. In fact, the signs are that real isolation and alienation are on the increase.

There are two kinds of lonely people — the circumstantially lonely who are newly out of their usual context — people on their own for the first time, students, the divorced, rejected, bereaved and so on. They need pointers on how to look out of a different window on the world and get a life. Their first steps out of loneliness are not too difficult: there are organizations, societies, clubs, classes and courses, community projects, work (paid and unpaid), meeting-places, pen-friends, helplines, dating and marriage agencies, lonely hearts ads — all practical first steps for anyone who really wants to make contact with others and is emotionally capable of doing so.

Then there are the temperamental loners — those who feel, all the time, that they're unacceptable outsiders, so undeserving of a place in the sun that they can't take any more steps out of their shell than are demanded by shopping and getting to and from work. They mostly manage to do this without making eye contact with anyone. In their company you feel oddly alone.

These self-absorbed loners range from teenagers to pensioners and are indeed lonely. As their anguished communications by post, phone, e-mail and internet testify, they're pleading with strangers to get them out. This is far more difficult to solve than the temporary loneliness of the circumstantial kind. In the end, if they really want to break out of their isolation they have to accept that no one is going to come beating at the door to ask: "Are you lonely?" And that they just have to take the first step themselves, even if it's only summoning up a smile and a "good morning" to the person they see regularly in a shop or bus queue or just across the way.

Now it seems that if you can only accept this simple truism that "it's up to me", the better you become at being alone without being lonely. Letters from older people experiencing loneliness showed they were more able to come to terms with it than younger people and often the case was that they merely wished to share, without moan or blame, the fact that they missed their children and grand-children and felt very keenly the loss of partners or long-time friends. They are also more open to a number of simple solutions — the idea, for instance, that other people are lonely too and that in going to places where other loners look for answers you could make a friend by being one.

What stops being alone turning into loneliness? Well, it's a psychological fact that it's not the amount of love you actually have in your life at this very moment that's important but how loved you feel in the depths of your being. That's why it behoves society as a whole to help every child to feel secure, confident and potentially lovable. What's more, we owe it to each other as adults to make other people feel they matter.

We can also acquire lovability for ourselves. Love and loving are not confined in any way. They are free-flowing and can inhabit us without living proof of their existence. Though we're all ultimately alone, and some day most of us will have to live without daily companionship and regular hugs, we can continue to feel loved through happy memories, contact with family and friends, being interested in life, learning and listening, helping people, giving time and love where we can, treating ourselves often, chiding ourselves less and checking any tendency to worry about what other people think of us.

If you have doubts about love's value, to both the giver and the receiver, here's a modern, real-life parable that might convince you. When the black teenager Stephen Lawrence lay dying in a London street, a woman who was passing stopped and bent down to cradle his head in her arms. Having been told that hearing was the last of our faculties to die, she whispered in his ear: "You are loved" — a truly marvellous thing to do. I don't know who the woman was, but I have the feeling that she was no youngster. It takes quite a lot of living to understand how important love is to all of us, how unimportant sex is by comparison and how loneliness can always be conquered.

GORDON MACPHERSON

Health questions, genetic answers

"I'm sorry, Mrs Clark, as you're over sixty you cannot have physiotherapy treatment for your back on the NHS. You can, however, be referred for private physiotherapy, which costs about £25 a session."

This is the gist of what an NHS general practitioner recently told a pensioner with backache caused by a longstanding bone disorder. I have changed her name, but she lives in an area which has many pensioners and where the traditional description of the NHS as a free and comprehensive service will ring a mite hollow. The doctor, I am sure, is competent and caring. In effect, he was delivering the message that in the area where this patient lived the NHS could no longer afford to treat all patients who need treatment.

So what's new? you may ask. After all, dialysis treatment for kidney disease has not been universally available for people over sixty-five for some time. And the media regularly carry stories of patients — young as well as old — who fail to get appropriate treatment or who have to wait many months to get it. What angered me was that Mrs Clark, who was a few months past sixty, was told that if she had been under sixty physiotherapy on the NHS would have been available. This policy may be widespread but, to me, it is planned discrimination against older people, and as someone of seventy I will no doubt be a victim of it sooner or later.

Admittedly, covert rationing — *pace* those Whitehall spin doctors who prefer that ugly word "prioritization" — has long been a part of the NHS. The service has been short of resources since it was launched fifty years ago and, though funding has historically increased at a much higher rate than overall inflation, resources have failed to keep pace with the rising costs of medical advances. Couple these costs with those of modernizing outdated buildings and the financial consequences of a steadily increasing proportion of older people in the population and it is no surprise the NHS cannot meet its original objective of a free, comprehensive service for all. Nevertheless, I object to a rationing system that penalizes a section of the community least able to afford fees for health care. Furthermore, most are people who have paid taxes throughout their lives and assumed they would not have the anxieties of paying for medical treatment in retirement. That was a fear that the NHS was intended to abolish.

I just hope the government's public acknowledgement of NHS rationing in the shape of national and local bodies to prepare guidelines on priorities will result in policies that do not penalize older people. It will be essential for pensioners, who form a substantial proportion of the voting, taxpaying community, to make their views known to these new policy bodies, nationally and locally. The national body for England and Wales is the National Institute for Clinical Excellence; that for Scotland is the Scottish Health Technology Assessment Centre.

This may not be the place for a polemic about the Mrs Clarks of this world having a moral, if not a legal, right to appropriate health care. But is a paradoxical that as medicine advances — perhaps "evolves" would be a more appropriate verb — more people are given longer lives during which they may suffer more age-related disorders for which the state may be unable or unwilling to provide tax-funded treatment. That paradox must be resolved if those of us in retirement now or in years to come are to enjoy reasonable lives free from worries about the financial consequences of ill health. Clever medicine will be of little use to those who cannot afford it.

So what should we do? A recent Royal Commission on the funding of long-term care for the elderly, though packed with fascinating facts, did not produce an answer. Indeed, according to Professor Elaine Murphy, writing in the *British Medical Journal* in early 1999, the commission failed "to make a visionary leap, [harking] back to a welfare philosophy of 50 years ago". That suggests that a credible solution is unlikely. As an alternative what I would like to suggest is a good dose of self-help. This may not be popular in an era when personal responsibility is out of fashion and finding someone to blame and sue for what is often life's natural hazards is a spreading habit. But older people can do quite a lot to keep themselves fit, while younger people can take straightforward and inexpensive measures to enhance their chances of ageing successfully.

Age is not a twenty-first-century phenomenon. It has achieved prominence as a political and medical issue because the proportion of elderly people in many countries has been rising steadily, as have overall population sizes. Surprisingly, 20 per cent of our hunter/gatherer ancestors survived until their sixties — infancy was the most dangerous period of their lives — and classical history is well endowed with venerable characters. I read recently of an eighty-five-year-old Spartan military leader who successfully headed an overseas expedition. Perhaps hunting and war provided the right balance of diet and exercise to ensure longevity — providing you weren't eaten by a carnivore or speared by an opponent, of course.

State intervention in the care of older people started in Elizabethan times. In pre-Tudor England the poor, the sick and the elderly were commonly cared for by religious institutions. After Henry VIII ravaged the monasteries many on society's fringes ended up on the streets, and the resulting social unrest prompted Elizabeth I's government to introduce the first Poor Law to provide basic social, health and educational facilities for the underclasses. A framework of parish-based and funded "workfare" services, including support for the elderly poor, was set up. Roy Porter, a medical historian, has described this first state intervention in health and social care as "nationalization of religious charity in the post-Reformation Protestant State".

That sixteenth-century experiment in nationalization resonated down the years, for when the NHS was set up in 1948 some of the hospitals it inherited had been built by local authorities which had administered the (much reformed) Poor Law. These institutions cared for many frail and elderly people. Sadly, not all were well run, and I believe that this reinforced the traditional disdain shown by many Victorians to the workhouse. This attitude lingered on in the NHS during its early days, contributing to the feeling among some health professionals, and indeed society generally, that the elderly were somehow second-class citizens. That unacceptable attitude can still be found.

When I first entered general practice in the late 1950s the local hospital for older people, especially those with chronic ailments, was a former workhouse. Patients admitted there rarely returned home, and treatment was mainly basic nursing. Then an innovative consultant physician was appointed who believed in treating and rehabilitating older patients and returning them home, arranging hospital day care when necessary. He believed they should be treated like patients from any other age group. The policy greatly improved the prospects of these older people, freed hospital beds so that GPs could more easily admit those patients who needed care and was a remarkable demonstration of what the emerging speciality of geriatrics was capable of achieving.

This conversion of a workhouse into an effective working hospital showed that the disorders suffered by older people were broadly similar to those occurring in people of all ages. However, older people tend to respond differently to sickness and to the treatments given. Drugs, for instance, are metabolized and excreted more slowly than in young adults. Ageing is associated with a progressive decline in the functioning of major organs such as the heart, lungs, kidneys and brain; infections of these organs are commonly life-threatening. Illness also slows the thinking of older people, often making them confused. Such organically induced confusion must not be mistaken for dementia, which results from the degeneration of brain cells. This is a not uncommon mistake that can result in an elderly patient receiving quite the wrong management with damaging consequences not only for the patient but also for the relatives.

The environmental influence on how long we live starts from the day of conception: the mother's state of health, the progress of her pregnancy, the socio-economic conditions into which the baby is born, the child's diet and the exercise it takes, as well as the care and affection provided by the parents — are all factors influencing the future adult's health. Subsequently the adult's lifestyle will affect not only their health during adulthood but their longevity and health in old age. For example, diet, the amount of exercise taken and smoking and drinking habits will all play a part.

For those already in retirement any consequences of their earlier lifestyles, including key events such as bereavement, divorce, unemployment, financial stress and premature retirement, may be mitigated but not necessarily overcome by adopting a different, healthier lifestyle. The scale of the problem, however, is great.

Surveys looking into the use of exercise have shown that around 40 per cent of all men and women aged fifty or over were sedentary (taking less than thirty minutes of exercise a week of sufficient intensity to benefit their health). Only one in four men and one in six women in this age group were frequently active (engaging in thirty minutes of intense activity at least five times a week). Whatever their past lifestyles, however, the elderly can improve their likelihood of successful ageing if they:

- eat sensibly, avoiding junk foods
- do not smoke
- drink modestly

- take regular exercise
- maintain or increase social contacts and activities
- keep mentally active.

Obviously, as with younger generations, the health of the elderly is sensitive to their socio-economic status. Poor diet, poor housing and a lack of domestic or community facilities for exercise and social contacts are not conducive to successful ageing. Sadly, those living in a poor environment are often the least responsive to advice on how to improve their lifestyles.

Many of us are fortunate to have a reasonable standard of living, though pensioners may be adept at disguising deteriorating financial circumstances. Nevertheless, walking, climbing stairs, step exercises, etc., are inexpensive ways of taking exercise, and much valuable advice on exercise and on balanced dieting is available through books, television and so on. In the USA, where lifestyle seems to be taken more seriously than in the UK, the incidence of strokes has fallen by a third and that of death from heart disease by a quarter in recent years. In Britain we are beginning to follow this trend, and experts suggest that early in the twenty-first century we could achieve an average life expectancy of eighty-five years.

While inheritance, living standards and lifestyle are crucial factors in successful ageing, medicine has contributed to people's longevity by more effective treatment of once potentially lethal diseases. High blood pressure, diabetes, kidney failure, many cancers, pneumonia and other infections and, of course, fractured bones can all be either controlled or cured. Disabling, if not always lethal, disorders such as Parkinson's disease, cataracts, deafness, epilepsy, skin diseases and arthritis are also curable or controllable. Mental disorders are often more difficult to treat, but great progress has been made in using drugs to mitigate or cure depression, a common illness among the elderly. One distressing condition is still generally resistant to medical intervention: dementia, with Alzheimer's disease its worst manifestation because it tends to strike early. Alzheimer's continues to ravage the over-sixty-fives, and in the UK around forty people a day are diagnosed as having the disease.

Illness can be devastating to the older person: apart from the disease's symptoms it may result in reduced mobility and increased social isolation. It also places a burden on relatives, if indeed there are any willing or able to help. Providing suitable care is perhaps the most intractable problem for the million or so disabled elderly people. Working wives, divorce and second marriages and the demands of modern employment on families mean that many old people cannot depend on relatives for help. Furthermore, local social service departments have tight budgets for organizing care, and people willing to work as carers are not in plentiful supply. The cost of retirement or nursing home places is such that many individuals and families cannot afford them without help.

Traditionally, old age has been equated with ill health, and the ability of modern medicine to cure or control many illnesses and to replace "faulty parts" has led to old age becoming medicalized. It seems that every ailment, however trivial, requires consultation with a doctor. Relatives with a trying grandparent too readily expect the NHS to sort out the problem. Families and communities seem to be losing the self-reliance that was a characteristic of my grandparents' generation. Somehow, and it won't be easy, we must promote the concept of self-help first and hold off seeking medical advice unless self-help fails or the illness obviously requires immediate medical intervention.

Schools and adult education courses should teach much more about healthy living: far better for tomorrow's grannies and grandpas to have prevented illness in old age instead of having to have it treated. The media have done a major service, as have organizations such as Help the Aged and Age Concern, by providing information and advice on diets, exercise programmes and other preventive measures. I would like government and the health professions to put as much effort into preventing illness — in all age groups — as they do into running the (largely) curative NHS. Investment in preventive medicine should pay immense social medical and economic dividends, albeit over a long period of time. And don't tell me politicians work to five-year timetables.

The over-sixty-fives are a substantial part of the population. They have the time, the skills and the election votes to campaign — locally and nationally — for a preventive approach to the objective of successful ageing for all. Apart from its worthy objective, such a campaign would provide the many older people capable of productive activity with increased opportunities of socializing and seeing themselves as useful members of the community instead of geriatric nuisances.

Looking to the future, it is clear that genetic science has been progressing at a startling pace. It will not be long before the position and functions of each one of the body's 100,000 genes — the hereditary units present in every body cell — will be known. In the next thirty years (or sooner) we can expect genetic manipulation of human embryos to be routine. Inherited disorders could be well nigh eliminated, and the body's characteristics — for instance, height, muscular strength, intelligence, etc. — could be enhanced by adding appropriate genes. Genes that make a person liable to develop cancer would be removed. There might be unexpected side-effects since nature is nothing if not unpredictable. Even so, there is a good chance that scientists will overcome many of the drawbacks of ageing: skin would maintain its youthful elasticity, men would keep their hair, joints would remain mobile and replacement tissues could be cultured to replace failing parts.

All this would put Aldous Huxley's Brave New World just around the corner. Personally, I am unlikely to see round it, and perhaps many people over sixty would prefer not to. But these genetic possibilities could lead to our grandchildren enjoying very successful ageing. They might even live to be 150 years old. Meanwhile in the prosaic present we must get down to our exercising, dietary planning, socializing and campaigning to mitigate the environmental handicaps we have unknowingly endured and make the best of our genetic longevity.

GETTING A LIFE

Angela Graham

Margaret Simey

Eric Midwinter

Peter Laslett

Barrie Porter

ANGELA GRAHAM

Into the void, and beyond

Not so long ago I became one among the thousands of newly retired people across the country enrolling for adult education classes. As we stood, waiting and idly chattering in rooms that catered for schoolchildren during the day, I fell to wondering what we were hoping for. Would the classes meet our uncertain needs, or would we soon give them up? Would we start looking for something else to fill the gap left by work?

What really happens to older people, I asked myself, when, for whatever reason, they leave paid employment. What do they do all day? How do they spend their time?

Pre-retirement courses may be proliferating, but are they really adequately preparing people for one of the biggest steps in their life? Usually, these courses place the emphasis on the positive aspects of retirement, pointing out all the things a retired person can do. The choice, they say, is infinite, ranging from part-time work, volunteering in all its diversity, to gardening, flower-arranging, delivering meals on wheels, and so on. The message is that no one should be bored.

Then there are those individuals who say: "There are the grandchildren." But this ignores the fact that many families these days are so widely scattered that grandchildren are not always an option or that some older people simply don't have any.

A film I saw at one pre-retirement course showed a couple a few weeks after the husband's enforced early retirement, rapidly adjusting to a situation where both appeared busy and happy with their various interests, shared and not shared. I wondered whether most people really adjust so quickly and so happily. The courses warn of the dire consequences of non-adjustment — ill health or even death. One result of this approach is that guilt becomes associated with an unhappy retirement and adds to the burden.

My father and my grandfather, I know, never got over the loss of the routine of their work. Both had continued in employment for as long as they could and, sadly, the time for them between retirement and death was not particularly happy. My mother and grandmothers, being housewives, did not have to face retirement themselves — only that of their spouses. So, for my generation of women, sixtyish and younger, there have been no female role models. We are breaking new ground.

I did not take to retirement easily. At least I am lucky: I do have family, friends and skills and am motivated enough to search for new and interesting things. But with the mandatory holiday in India accomplished, endless time — a vacuum — stretched ahead. I found that I was dwelling a great deal on what I had lost. Apart from the money coming in, I still missed the on-the-spot companionship, the humour of the office, sharing the trivia and drama of other people's lives — births, marriages, new jobs and even retirements. I was no longer part of that . . .

Retirement is a bereavement, but the courses I attended, though good on the subject of financial planning, for instance, devoted little time to the psychological and emotional aspects, the real sense of loss.

The colleagues I left behind are still busy coping with the demands and stresses of their jobs, and they may look on retired friends with a certain amount of envy. But maintaining relationships with them — keeping up with friends — is not always easy for any of us. They are busy, and those lunches, so valuable to me, are often difficult for them. The consequence is that friends gradually but imperceptibly fall away, and it is no one's fault.

In addition to the obvious losses that retirement brings — loss of role, of status, of the very activity of work, of income — there may be the adjustment to a partner who is also now at home. Very possibly, apart from weekends and holidays, the retired couple may not have spent that much time together. Suddenly they find they are spending whole days in each other's company.

It now seems that I constantly have to negotiate use of the car, the telephone, the bathroom or even having friends to lunch. My personal space has suddenly become very important, and when conflict arises there is no one to let off steam to except one's partner. The listening ear of a work colleague is no longer available. If such things are not seriously discussed and negotiated by partners, retirement can and will lead to marital conflict and even breakdown.

Single people, too, can have particular problems when they retire. They have often relied on work almost exclusively for companionship, and the loneliness of their single existence is brought home to them when the office or factory door is closed on them for the last time. The lucky ones have friendships and interests outside, but many are thrown back on their own resources. Even meals can be a problem when there is no partner to share with. One recently retired friend told me how she panicked when she felt she had been sitting in her chair for hours, though when she looked at her watch she found that only ten minutes had passed. Whole days can be spent alone, and the arrival of the postman, the e-mail or the odd telephone call are the only diversions.

The wish to move house, to start a new life, to be nearer children and grandchildren is common among the newly retired. I thought satisfying this want might fill the gap left by work and so I flooded estate agents with requests for "suitable" properties in my own neighbourhood or elsewhere. But then I faltered and with hindsight I now think that rushing into something as big as changing homes, without proper adjustment to retirement, would have been a mistake. Just as newly bereaved widows or widowers are advised to wait before thinking of moving, so should the newly retired.

Moving into an unfamiliar area can bring stresses as well as advantages. It may mean, for instance, the loss of friends as well as more casual acquaintances, like the man who says "Hello" when he's walking his dog. We forget too how much we depend on familiar shops (and shopkeepers), parks and cafés, to say nothing of services like those of our GP, dentist or even post office. We get a lot of advice on whether or not to move, but the best policy is probably to wait a while rather than rush into a decision we might later regret.

Grieving, all the experts tell us, is a process that has to be worked through, and, just as with any other loss, this is true of retirement. Depression, anger, frustration, disappointment and empty days are interspersed with relief and pleasure at doing what one likes, free from the restrictions and irritations of work. Some days I still wake up terrified at all the space and unstructured time, but on others I revel in the luxury and the prospect of idleness.

What helped me most in the weeks and months following retirement has been other people and especially those in a similar situation to my own.

When I did eventually join the right class — though I was reluctant at first to take the plunge — I found to my surprise that it was filled with people at or close to the same stage in their lives. They were warm and friendly and they generously welcomed me to their group. Week by week, as I sat in this class, I felt encouraged — by one of the best teachers I ever had. As I chatted with my fellow students I felt a surge of relief and excitement that there were, after all, people out there whom I could talk to and whose company I could enjoy.

Friends from my pre-retirement days have tended to sort themselves out — into those who understand and those who don't. At one stage I made a conscious decision to let some people go and to concentrate on those whom I could still really talk to and with whom I could share my new life. As work fades, having friends who are also retired, sharing coffee, evenings out, weekends or holidays has become increasingly important. Pressure on one's partner, or children, is eased if there are other people with whom one can share things. Effort is required, but I am now convinced that such new relationships are very significant for the mental health of the retired.

Having a "project" can help to alleviate the feelings of uselessness and worthlessness people often feel when they retire. With this in mind, I searched hard for something worth while to do. I had to find myself again. What sort of person was I? What were my skills? What did I enjoy doing? This process took time, and the search was not without its disappointments. Promises were not always kept, and my confidence in negotiating a role for myself in the world of voluntary or semi-voluntary work needed boosting. I am convinced there was an element of ageism in the responses that I received from some of the projects which I considered, and I was hurt at times that my skills could be ignored because I did not have the backing of an organization. I am still looking . . .

At first I was tempted to do too much. To avoid those empty days I booked into lots of classes, tore up and down motorways visiting people and places, met individuals I really wanted to see less of. Then I realized that — just as at work — it was I myself who had to sort out my priorities, decide what was important, what I enjoyed and what I could discard. At first it was quite scary to have so much time and no one but myself to do the organizing. At the age of sixty, for the first time in my life I was accountable only to myself.

The onus of responsibility for how I spend my time rests with me alone. In practical terms, this means a lot of decision-making. It takes time to get used to being retired and to re-engage with the world in a new way. It does not happen without causing some pain and upheaval, even though I once longed for the day when paid work would finish. There is that vacuum to fill, and roles in family and community have to be redefined. For me, this adjustment has been as big as when I gave up work to have my first child.

People need to be gentle with themselves and mourn the loss of their previous life. They need time to talk, to exchange views and feelings. It is a great comfort to find a friend in a similar situation, but this is not always possible and isolation can compound the problem. I would recommend the setting-up of post-retirement groups, meetings and classes at which men and women can come together to share real concerns. For most, individual counselling and therapy are not necessary, but they could become so if the problem is not acknowledged and addressed. I would hope that in future the appropriate organizations will put as much of their energies into post-retirement support as now goes into pre-retirement courses.

Postscript: I am now nearly three years into retirement, and at last the vacuum appears to have been filled. The temptation now is to take on too much and leave too little time and space to stop, relax and even dream. I have to fight the Protestant work ethic and to tell myself that I don't have to fill the day with worthwhile activities. After all, I spent the last forty years doing just that.

MARGARET SIMEY

How, and where, I found independence

Independence! There's a daydream if ever there was one. All my life I have hankered after it. To be free to be myself. Not to be free of family or friends whom I dearly love but to be free from being cabined and confined by what is expected of me. Like the old dame in Jenny Joseph's rightly popular poem, I long to be free to wear purple with a red hat that doesn't "go" with it if I feel like it. Instead of which, my life has been cluttered with assumptions imposed on me by other people.

As a girl in a family that seemed to consist entirely of men — bar my mother, of course — I knew from birth what was expected of me. At school I was put in the B stream because I was thought to be second-class material and had to be educated accordingly — an assumption I meekly accept to this day, even though I have written books and have been awarded an honorary degree by Liverpool University on the strength of them. When I married, the clamps were well and truly put in place; my mother-in-law saw to that. She could make the most dream-like of meringues stuffed with fresh cream, and I had to do the same. The university where my husband worked assumed that now I was married I would no longer pursue my career as a youth worker. And so on and on, until the day came when our young ones had left home and my husband died. Surely now I could, at last, be me?

Not a bit of it. By happy chance, having been recruited by the women's emancipation movement in the 1920s and having been an active politician ever since, I had got away with being an ordinary member of society regardless of age, running from meeting to meeting just like anybody else. But then some kind but misguided persons laid on a surprise birthday party when I was ninety. I don't know who was more surprised — me or the guests. Until then they had called me Old Indestructible, so I was told, but now they realized that I was Old. I was promptly shifted into a different category. Overnight their behaviour towards me changed dramatically. Do you need a chair, dear? Would you like a cup of tea, love? Most cruel of all, whatever would I do with myself now that I was retired?

My previous life as an ordinary citizen came to an abrupt end. To be Old is by definition to be pitiable, and poor, to suffer from irreversible decrepitude, to be doomed to go to the workhouse — or to "a home". As befits my new status as a member of the cohorts of the dependent, I must keep my head down, stop clamouring for a better pension, be grateful for my free bus pass and for concessions when I go into a museum, though I sometimes think I would be more properly on display as an exhibit than visiting as a spectator.

The whole welfare system seems hell-bent on keeping me in what "they" think is my proper place. A recent hip replacement brought home to me my lack of independence. In hospital, when I asked for a hot drink at bedtime it was refused as being contrary to the caterer's contract — though to the credit of the nursing profession hot Horlicks magically arrived nevertheless. Then I discovered that a weekly case conference was held to review the progress of myself and all patients on the ward; this would decide when I would be allowed to go home. But I was excluded from this — it was evidently nothing to do with me. When they suggested I should go to a convalescent home, I panicked. I felt that if I agreed that would be the end of my independence. I insisted on going home, and, with the admirable care of community services, I survive.

What is so very exasperating is that none of this is inevitable. Ageism is a strictly European phenomenon, a comparatively recent by-product of the industrial conurbation society. In that context, as non-workers, older people are a drag on the market, of no value, a cost and a problem. There is no scope in the marketplace for those officially declared redundant by reason of chronological age. Nor, in this era of short-term contracts, is there any background stability, no family into whose life the ageing can comfortably subside as frailty catches up. And, once we have been reduced to dependence, our existence is resented as an expense that society cannot afford even it wanted to. Is there really no alternative? Must I just resign myself to sitting on a beach in Spain until the time comes to retreat into that "home" to wait interminably for death to come?

My answer came from Africa — as wisdom so often does, if only we had the humility to listen. On a visit to my son in Lesotho, the land-locked little kingdom embedded in southern Africa, I found myself greeted with immense enthusiasm by the villagers. Pleased but baffled by my reception, I was told on inquiry that what moved them to such a display was their pleasure that my son should enjoy the exceptional good fortune of having such a very old mother. To them, my experience and wisdom were worth more than money in the bank.

My son's relationship with me underwent a subtle change, but the effect on me was little short of a revelation. My hitherto vague yearning after an undefined state of independence came sharply into focus. The poverty-stricken villagers, whom I patronizingly supposed I had come to help, had in fact turned the tables on me. They made me realize that what I meant by independence was that I wanted to be a person in my own right. I wanted to be of value because I was me, because I was old and not in spite of it. I was tired of being allocated a slot in life as somebody else's mother or wife or daughter. I just wanted to be an upright, self-respecting individual who existed in my own right — an elder of the tribe. To be free of other people's assumptions, to decide for myself what sort of life I would lead. That would be independence.

It is tantalizingly easy to spend time drawing up a shopping-list of what could and should be done if those who are growing older are to be set free from the subtle form of discrimination that is ageism. There must be an end to the whole silly business of a universal and compulsory retirement age fixed to suit the requirements of the insurance industry. The government, for its part, must overcome the national obsession with work as the remedy for all ills. (Who will employ me in my nineties?)

Certainly, old age pensioners are in need of a better income, but money won't buy the status and security as respected members of the community of which older people are consistently deprived. Better housing, a revised pension scheme, a social wage for those who have done their stint in the marketplace but who now want to play their part in the wider community . . . All these, and more, add up to a formidable list.

In our hearts, we know all too well that these are daydreams. We have seen too many royal commissions and reports come and go for us to be other than cynical. Never in our lifetime will we live to see more than a tenth of what ought to be done to alleviate the burden of ageism — if for no other reason than the stark fact that as a society we simply cannot afford to go on in the manner to which we are accustomed, let alone improve on it. In other words, our choice is limited.

But either we go on doing as we did before but ever more cheaply, snipping pennies and pounds off the services we already provide till they dwindle away to extinction, or — and this is a far more exciting prospect — we bravely take a totally fresh look at our entire approach to the question of the role and responsibilities of the older section of the community. Instead of regarding older people as a burdensome responsibility, we must adopt a policy based on regard for them as our betters and as a social asset and not as a liability.

Such a tremendous change in attitude is the clue to progress in the future. Given that, the sky's the limit — without it we stagnate, saddled with a mass of dependants whose existence will undermine all our dreams of becoming a caring community. The Welfare State will take from us all the hope of ever becoming a Welfare Society.

To start with — and this is absolutely fundamental to the strategy of change — there must be a determined onslaught to raise ageism awareness. It must be recognized for what it is: as one of the splendid people at the Open University puts it, "a peculiar form of social oppression", one of the most subtle of the many hidden discriminations that disfigure our society. In its place must be put the positive concept of the senior sector of the community as the older members of the tribe. The implications of such a concept in the changed and changing society of today have never been thought through.

The value in community terms of the experience of older people is never subjected to anything other than an economic audit. There is no appreciation of the literal value of older people in maintaining the continuity of traditions and values which are essential in the fight against the break-up of traditional family life. Little girls come with tape recorders to learn about the days when old people were young, but it is a scandal that the teaching of social history is no longer regarded as worthy of a place in the school curriculum. Similarly, further education fails lamentably to offer training in the true value and fulfilment of the duties of older people.

It won't be easy. To effect a change in ingrained habits of thought is extraordinarily difficult — as the police are now learning with much pain and grief. But the entire population must in effect be re-educated, from children to OAPs. The bevy of gallant "grey" movements must set their sights far higher than the demand for increased pensions.

Quite the most difficult obstacle of all will be the entrenched battalions of bureaucrats and professionals who are the custodians of institutionalized ageism. They exist to administer the status quo without fear or favour, not to change it. Though nominally without power, they nevertheless exercise a stranglehold over any advance in social policy. Instead of regarding the older sector they exist to serve as a burdensome liability, they must set about devising means of treating them as an asset of immense potential. There is much to learn from the police, who openly talk of themselves as a force and not a public service.

Even so, I am optimistic. The sheer irrelevance of what passes for a policy for the third sector is actually making itself evident to those in authority as well as to the supposed beneficiaries. There are signs of comprehension on the part of the public in general that a social policy based on economic principles is neither effective nor efficient. It is this groundswell of opinion that current practice is simply not acceptable that will ultimately move the mountain of institutional opposition to change.

One last word of caution. There is a danger that a wave of support for change will in practice mean a jump from the frying-pan into the fire. It is not desirable that a policy of social inclusion should be so thorough-going as to constitute a wholesale takeover of the management of common affairs by the establishment, nor that the growing enthusiasm for "participation" should subject the elderly to patronage by an executive class who will kindly invite them to come and play in their playground — on their terms, of course — for they will firmly retain their grip on the levers of control.

If such difficulties are to be circumvented, all those who labour to promote an advance in social policy regarding older people will have to learn to rely ever more humbly on the wisdom of the tribal elders. A vision perhaps, but for lack of a vision the people perish.

Eric Midwinter

Education — bus or tram?

There once was a man who said, "Damn!
It is borne in upon me I am
An engine that moves
In predestinate grooves;
I'm not even a bus, I'm a tram."
— Maurice Hare

We are all creatures of our social and cultural environment, inheritors of its prejudices and attitudes. We may not be trams driven along the lines ordained by supernatural forces of fate or providence, but we are certainly conveyed, often unwittingly and ingenuously, along the route signposted by our cultural values. In every study of factors in educational performance, the home and neighbourhood outgun the school, for better or for worse, in the ratio of roughly four to one. It's not five-nil — the school and college do have some influence — but then schools are themselves part of society, with teachers as much affected by the prevailing norms as anyone else.

162

Society determines the way we view old age; worse, it can dictate the way old people view old age. We have been educated since the dawn of humankind that oldness equals illness, that it is about being over the hill and no longer a contributor to socio-economic life. Forget the myths of a golden past or of mystical other societies where old people were or are treated with enormous dignity and respect. In every community there has ever been, old people have, by and large, been regarded ambivalently, with a volatile mix of niceness and nastiness.

Sometimes we care for old people; sometimes we think they are a bloody nuisance; it could be the same old person in the same ten minutes. That's why the mayor visits the local residential care home on Christmas Day — to compensate for all those other days when we care much less. That's why, if the public's response to charitable appeals was structured like a football league table, old age charities would be in a mid-table position, with guide dogs for the blind and lifeboatmen fighting it out for a place in Europe and with released convicts and drug addicts struggling against relegation.

Advertising is a picturesque example of our cultural and educative ambiance. Advertisers rarely invent images; they have so little time. They merely play back to us versions of the images that are already in our educated heads. You never see old women advertising shower gel or deodorant, but you may find them boosting the sales of brown

163

bread and soup. When the gallant hero goes through hell and high water, it's always his girlfriend who gets the chocolates — never his granny or his mother-in-law.

Our culture is replete with myths of failing and deterioration in old age. Since at least the time of Chaucer the joke about the scrawny, impotent old man and the nubile up-for-it young girl has done the rounds. Think of those lethal proverbs and adages: "You can't teach an old dog new tricks"; "Mutton dressed as lamb"; or the expressive seventeenth-century way of describing an old woman in bright clothes: "Like a wanton song at a funeral".

Unhappily, old people believe the propaganda. They indulge in what the pundits call "age-appropriate behaviours". Most of them act out the role of being old. That's what they have been taught to do. Some don't. Some climb mountains and run marathons. These are the ones you tend to hear about, the ones who claim: "Since I finished work, I seem busier than ever." The huge silent majority retire literally, dwelling resignedly in the antechambers of society. Though retired people have massive reservoirs of spare time — twice as much as working people — they are engaged less than younger people on every index of recreational activity, except telly-watching, where they notch up an average of almost forty hours a week. Incidentally, when they themselves are used in television, old people are often comic or dismal figures, deployed to reflect by comparison the heroic and glamorous qualities of younger characters.

The brilliant community physician, John Muir Gray, has clinically demonstrated the notion of the "fitness gap", the fissure that widens as you grow older between what you can do and what you actually do, socially and intellectually as well as physically. Moreover, he asserts that a major reason for this is the cultural imperative that old people must behave as they feel is expected of them, with much slowing down and stopping of doing things. This is on a par with finding after finding, on both sides of the Atlantic, that old people regard education as something for the young and that learning is something that becomes more difficult with increasing age. After all, we live in a culture where, if a young person forgets something, it's a slip or lapse of memory, whereas, for an old person, "my memory's going". Ours is a culture where words like "senile" and "gaga" are used indiscriminately (and, in the case of "geriatric", ungrammatically). It is true that a fifth of people over eighty have some form of dementia, and we should act swiftly and resourcefully to grapple with that nightmare — but it would be nice to hear an occasional cheer for the four-fifths of people over eighty who haven't.

What is even more unfortunate is that this traditionally negative approach to old age persists at a time when old age, in the social sense of freedom from work and mainline child-rearing duties, is fast becoming the predominant arc in the lifespan. The

165

idea of the short retirement as a kind of ultimate holiday with pay, along with a nice little bungalow outside Morecambe or a little allotment near Chesterfield, has vanished. We are getting close to the fifty-year retirement for the centenarian who finishes work, as many do, in his or her early fifties. Some 12 million citizens of the UK and 80 million in the European Community are in their Third Age: that is a quarter of the adult population. By 2020 there will be as many people over sixty in the world — one billion — as there were people of any age in 1840.

The trouble is that a time-lag has developed between the new reality and the old "educated myth" of old age. The standard retirement course may concentrate on telling people how to resolve questions of finance, health, housing and the like. They present a static picture for people who have often had dynamic lives, moving jobs and houses, changing partners, getting promoted and all the rest of it. Now they are severely told, if only by implication, to find their rut and stick to it, with little sense of the necessity for finding a new time-map for another journey of thirty, forty, even fifty years. The best retirement course, in my experience, is the one where clients begin by listing what they hate about work, concentrating on the compelling joys to come.

Society requires a basic re-education in what it means to be older today and tomorrow. The cultural bells must change their tune, so that their chimes ring out a more resoundingly positive call. The new old age has not yet found its own narrators, composers, architects, designers and artists, an imaginative and harmonious team of campanologists to sound out the miracle of the late twentieth century; to wit, that we have discovered the trick of ensuring the most, not just a few, people now enjoy what we would regard as a wholesome, lengthy, natural lifespan. Of course, old people must get involved in what amounts to a cultural revolution. They must be to the fore in inventing the new institutions, agencies, art forms, designs, language, dress, music, artefacts and literature of which their lifestyle will be composed.

A primary consideration must be the acceptance of old people as citizens rather than social casualties. That is one of the most magnificent aspects of the University of the Third Age in Britain, run by and for old "lay" people and often in a member's home. Such activities proclaim the virtue of older citizens running their own affairs.

In the past we have lived with the sobering image of the professional officer delivering a service to the humble elderly recipient. Think of meals on wheels. Often that has amounted to indifferent fare, delivered at a time without consultation with the receiver, and, most chilling of all, the old person has been expected to be deferentially grateful for this mediocre bounty. Did someone mention the value of the social contact? One piece of research went so far as to suggest that the length of the average telephone call was just fourteen seconds.

The analogy of the bus and the tram which I quoted at the outset is an accurate one, certainly in cultural terms. Unlike the Calvinistic dictates of divine providence, social and cultural determinism is human-made, just like buses and trams. At the very minimum, we can decide to shift, lengthen or reverse the tram-lines. We have it within us to alter the perception of old age, and our society could begin to educate its members, not least its older members, in these new and better truths about the last third of life.

A splendid example of such cultural change is the public attitude to smoking. After the First World War, when the cigarette became widely used, smoking was the norm. Many will recall (since we are using public transport as a running metaphor) how much smoking there was on buses, trains and trams, as well as in cinemas. Now as a result of a compound of official strictures about health and a complete change in artistic presentation, smoking has become the oddity, banned on much of public transport and in most cinemas. You rarely see people smoking on television because the creators of programmes have heeded both the warnings and the newer reality that smoking is a minority sport. Society has learned to "educate" its citizenry afresh.

An arduous but enthralling challenge faces us. Most education is of backward-looking, time-worn content. It has truly been said that we educate our children as if they are going to become our grandparents — one of the reasons, by and by, that formal schooling is so unsuccessful in its hidden agenda of producing young adults whose values are congruent with those society likes to cherish. In future education, in this broadest of meanings, must turn its back on the past, precisely because circumstances have so radically changed. We have nothing to guide us from the past, simply because the concept of "the first mass leisure class" has never before arisen in human history. We must first create the educational curriculum before we begin the tuition. We must build a new tram and then decide in which direction to lay its lines.

PETER LASLETT

Aristotle and the Beatles

In many areas of life, what older people know and what they need to know are much the same as they are for younger people. But because the inevitable disadvantages of day-to-day living are more pronounced for older people, and sometimes even extreme, maintaining their stock of knowledge is a little difficult. In actual fact physical and mental decline begin — very, very gradually — as early as the late twenties, though they are hardly noticeable until two decades later and do not usually become much of a hindrance until two decades beyond that, in the seventies and eighties.

In normally healthy people there is not likely to be a real problem of dependency or of slowness of uptake, or even seriously defective memory, until this stage is reached, and then only a small minority are affected. Individuals on this final stretch are properly termed the "aged", and they are the main focus of the work of the organization we are celebrating in this book.

These elementary facts illustrate the reality of ageing and the need for an appropriate attitude to older people. They are emphatically not a society apart. They are simply us, people at large, grown older. In due course practically all of us will grow older, and we will be just like them.

This means that when we think of the knowledge that older people ought to have and the education that should be available to them, we should regard their situation and their needs as constituting a particular example of the circumstances surrounding everyone at every age. However, these circumstances are a historical novelty. No previous society has consisted of persons who could all reasonably expect to become old and who are also prepared to become very old. Never before has everyone had to rely on knowing as much as we all have to know or to confront the need to have that knowledge continuously brought up to date. If these things did not happen we could not be a "whole" society, with everyone communicating with everyone else and all of us understanding each other.

Under the circumstances in which we now live, any interruption of learning diminishes social solidarity, which means that those who are ignorant or out of date lose contact with their age-mates and their juniors. This can happen at any age but is much more likely in later life, and this in turn means that particular arrangements have to be made for seniors. They have to be kept in touch mostly, but not completely, by their juniors.

The traditional picture of instruction, therefore, in which teachers are knowledgeable older people who impart necessary information to younger people at a time when these younger people are learners, mostly still at the socialization stage of their lives while the old are simply out of the picture, is sadly incomplete and anachronistic. Nevertheless this is the picture that always comes to mind when education is being discussed, because it describes what goes on in our schools and other places of learning. Indispensable as these institutions are, they have for some time ceased to be the whole story, and they are largely irrelevant to those who wish to undertake or to encourage learning at an older age.

There is a very important further fact about the age relationship of the teacher and the taught. Individuals learn from each other at all periods of their lives, and it would seem that this mutual imparting and reinforcement of knowledge is particularly well marked during what is coming to be called the Third Age. Indeed the British Universities of the Third Age (U3A for short), all 350 or more of them, are learning "exchanges" where everyone teaches and everyone learns in small, entirely informal, face-to-face groups which they themselves set up, often in members' houses. You are rewarded for teaching a subject to one group, teaching which has to be as up to date as you can make it, by yourself being taught another subject by someone else in another group. Money therefore never changes hands.

Addresses are also delivered to larger gatherings of members of a U3A, usually the whole body of them, by acknowledged experts in possession of the latest information. Such authoritative speakers are mostly still in jobs and not likely to count themselves as being in the Third Age. Money does come into it here, since fees have to be available for them as they are outside the learning exchange. The modest annual subscriptions of U3A members suffice for this purpose and for the hiring of premises, which are the main expenses. Incidentally, people in the Second Age (which is that of work, earning and production) are often generous to the older members of the population and regularly give their services without charge.

Finally, in this effort to keep the knowledge of every member intact and up to date, U3As are encouraged to maintain relationships with individuals who have become house-bound or institutionalized (who may be defined as having entered the Fourth Age) and to do everything possible to sustain and improve their current stock of information. Such people naturally tend to be older than the general run of Third Agers, and teaching them clearly has to bear this in mind.

The characteristically British system of mutual learning — characteristic because it is essentially amateur — is obviously of considerable importance when one considers the question of educating the old and the very old. This system is highly economical both because salaries do not have to be found for teachers and because it can make use of the large reserve of knowledge and experience possessed by former professional educators as well as other sorts of expertise which the retired already have. It reaches parts that other organizations cannot reach since U3As can be set up anywhere, irrespective of the available educational resources. What is more, it gives older people their own institutions, founded and entirely run by themselves. This makes them more effective, adds to their status and raises their and others' awareness of their social position.

However, the U3A model has its disadvantages because nearly all older people regard a university — any university — as quite outside, indeed above, the realm of their own experience. They find it too formidable to contemplate teaching anybody anything in such a context. This is to some extent due to the elitist tradition of "higher" education in Britain, which is a barrier to any sort of reform but which may be weakening now that so many new universities have come into being.

As I argued in my book *A Fresh Map of Life*, Britain is one of the least suited of the advanced countries to undergo the ageing transformation because of the character of our class divisions which have made themselves apparent in educational matters. But it is less of an ordeal than many might think to talk to a group in a British U3A. This is because it is the members who decide on standards and subjects, and they welcome any offer of a topic which is capable of interesting, informing and helping people like themselves.

Offerings are frequently based on the job expertise acquired during the Second Age by the would-be member-teacher. This means there are groups in subjects such as accountancy, architecture and the law or in computing (very popular) but also in ornithology, local history, languages (ever more popular, from French to classical Greek), not to speak of the fine arts of every kind — painting, music, dance and theatre (here the class becomes the *dramatis personae*). The list is surprisingly long, even in the small U3As, and they can be as small as seventy to a hundred members.

Handicrafts are very popular — woodworking, tapestry/weaving and even bridge — though there is some controversy over whether such subjects rightly belong to the curriculum or whether they should be classed among the many sporting and recreational activities in which members of the U3As enthusiastically engage. Some critics are now saying that the more exacting principles, like that of every member being prepared to teach or the matter of maintaining contact with those in the Fourth Age, are scarcely respected in some U3As.

As must be expected under British conditions, very few members of the U3As come from outside the middle class or even from outside the minority of that class which is intellectually disposed. This might be seen as a clinching argument against believing that the principles and practices of U3A could teach the whole population what they need to know throughout their lives. However, a couple of points should be borne in mind.

The British U3As were set up to introduce a new principle into late life learning. They were not intended to replace existing teaching facilities that are open to older people, such as adult education classes or the Open University, an earlier venture which came from the same innovatory stable and which remains extremely important to U3A programmes. Moreover there is still room for other non-intellectual organizations to arise, perhaps from within the U3A, though not necessarily as part of it. These might cater for the interests of others in the population, especially the working class and younger people.

What is clear is that the conventional model of education in which all teaching is done by Second Age professionals is simply too expensive to meet the needs of our knowledge-based society. When so much is being said about the enormous cost of providing for the livelihood and health of the great and growing community of the retired, their educational needs come a long way down the list.

Nevertheless, we are facing a menace to the very fabric of our society. The body politic could fall apart, to be replaced by a succession of age groups socialized at different points in the past, each holding fast to their different and out-of-date techniques, knowledge and attitudes. Given that Second Age values now enjoy undisputed sovereignty in our society, and yet the Second Age is on the way to becoming a minority of the adult population because of the ageing transformation, it could be argued that this social dissolution is already happening.

One last warning is in order. The current, and laudable, drive towards life-long learning is not really facing up to the fundamental issues, especially in relation to cost. It is also misguided in that it is confined to instilling knowledge that is interesting and useful predominantly to Second Age users — knowledge that is professional, technical or scientific in character. The long years now being spent in the Third Age, which will become even longer in the future, additionally require the universal diffusion of humane learning in everything from Aristotle and the Bible to Betjeman and the Beatles. Statesmen, education authorities, legislators, experts on ageing: please take note.

BARRIE PORTER

Untangling the net

If you have managed to reach, or pass, the age of sixty without having used a computer, it may be hard to convince you there is any point in starting now. Indeed, you may be one of that dying breed never to have used a computer, while the generation following you into retirement will have taken technology in its stride.

On the other hand, here you are, with the prospect of more time ahead and an inclination to learn a new skill. If you feel sufficiently motivated, the world is your oyster. If you plan to do any freelance work, communicating with an employer from your new workplace — your home — will be far more efficient if you do not have to rely on the post or the telephone. Don't be intimidated by the technology. I have looked on with amazement as my wife has converted from being very anti-computer to a state where every day she reels off letters, posters and spreadsheets with a degree of competence that she can be proud of. In her case, committee work, organizing events and keeping in touch with family and friends provided the motivation.

You may be right to be cynical about how useful a computer can be in the home. Who wants to turn it on to look up a telephone number? But if you look upon it as a hobby you might enjoy, you stand a chance of not being disappointed. My own computer, bought when I retired several years ago, is still keeping me amused. You don't have to keep buying new ones, though you may have to update bits here and there.

Once you have acquired your own machine, getting to know each other should be taken quite slowly. Unless you live in the depths of the countryside you will almost certainly have access to a wide choice of courses for students at all stages of computing. But even here you may meet an unexpected hurdle. How, other than by personal recommendation from other students, can you possibly assess which is the right course for you? In my view, you need to start with a working knowledge of the machine's potential. One hears, though, of courses where too much time is taken up with this, while the student is straining at the leash to progress to the interesting bit — producing some results. Conversely, there are instructors who plough straight into the exciting stuff, leaving their students no wiser about the nature of the intimidating beasts before them.

A better way might be to search around for a sympathetic friend, who (ideally) is also retired and who has the time and patience to take you through the various stages at a leisurely pace. That way you can call the tune, taking as long as you wish to master one step before proceeding to the next. With luck, your friend will be at the end of a telephone if you inadvertently press the wrong key and become totally stuck. Your computer whizzkid offspring is probably not the most suitable person to instruct you, incidentally. His or her incredulity at the aged parent's snail-like progress will increase at a rate similar to that of your own sense of abject failure. No, a contemporary is the person you need.

Having negotiated this initial hurdle, and feeling fairly comfortable with your computer, you now encounter a second challenge. As with so many hobbies, it is easy to get hooked. We are used to the image of teenagers mesmerized by their computer games, with accompanying problems of eyestrain, poor posture, light deprivation and the like. A first-time computer owner of sixty-plus has the potential for developing a similar addiction, without the compensation of youthful speedy recovery. The purchase of "computer spectacles" may be considered advisable, essential even. Reading glasses, driving glasses, computer glasses . . . so how does one remember to have the right ones at the right time? More than once I have found myself two streets away from home, peering over the steering wheel through lenses designed for looking at a screen placed just eighteen inches from the end of my nose.

RSI, meanwhile, has become one the growing number of relevant acronyms. The letters stand for repetitive strain injury and refer to the pain from muscular damage which can follow long hours of sitting in the same position using the same keyboard movement. RSI was once treated, like gout, as something of a joke, but it is now regarded as a serious problem for which industrial compensation is often sought. There is no compensation, though, for the retired first-time computer enthusiast. Nor can any sympathy be expected from the long-suffering partner, who is torn between feeling aggrieved at being neglected in favour of the new toy and relieved that the computer buff is not any longer "getting under my feet".

A sensibly used computer can add a new dimension to practically any interest — writing letters, composing music, recording family trees, garden design, photography — but you need to explore for yourself what it can be made to do for you. The most common computer program is the word-processor, which acts like a glorified typewriter but is more tolerant of inexpert typing. This is closely followed by the spreadsheet, which allows a multitude of repetitive calculations to be carried out in a flash. Then comes the database, which lets you organize all sorts of information from addresses to zoological species and then lose it all by pressing the wrong button. Computers are very quick, especially when they know you've just made a mistake.

Personally, I think the computer comes into its own when it starts to link you up with other people. This may be through your providing a service for others — like designing notices for local groups. Once word spreads that you are willing to provide this service, just sit back and wait for the rush. There is a lot of satisfaction to be gained from notice and poster design, both aesthetically and from the service given to other people. You may be called upon to provide support for a friend's or relative's interests. We have spent many happy hours recycling photographs. If you have a scanner, you can "read" a picture into the computer and make a few subtle changes. That slightly risqué holiday snapshot can be recycled into a "caption competition" or "fill in the thinks bubble", making a highly personal greetings card. If you run into someone else who is exploring the computer world you can swap ideas. You can also strengthen your link with the younger generation: your grandchildren will regard you with new admiration when you reveal your skills and show that you understand how they are using computers at school.

The computer also provides you with a new means of direct communication with others — somewhere between writing conventional letters and ringing other people up. This electronic mail — e-mail for short — can combine the best of both worlds because like the telephone it is quick and easy, and there is no need to compose a complete letter — just get to the point. Like a letter, it is cheap and can be received anywhere anytime (for the price of a local call, even though it may be going to the other side of the world); the advantage is that it takes minutes rather than days to arrive. It really comes into its own if you have family or friends abroad: you can keep in touch on a daily basis without the overkill of an expensive telephone call which in any case often arrives at the wrong time of day — or night. Imagine sending a message to a friend in the Antipodes as you go to bed and having the reply waiting when you get up next morning.

The success of e-mail relies on finding others who are able and willing to communicate like this. In general, the e-mail does not announce its arrival; you have to look for it. This can become frustrating if you keep looking and never receive any messages. If you look only occasionally, then as a system it fails to get going. So you need to work at it on a regular basis, and then it can turn out to be very rewarding.

As with any other means of communication, e-mail has its own customs and idiosyncrasies. There is a new protocol to get used to. E-mail is considered by most users to be more similar to conversation than to letter-writing; punctuation and spelling are not seen as important — so do not think badly of a correspondent who breaks all the rules of grammar. A new kind of punctuation has evolved in the form of "emoticons", to signal in an e-mail the sort of meaning which would be self-evident in conversation. Most common is the smiley face :-), which is used to indicate a comment not intended to be taken too seriously, such as "Wish you were here." Writing e-mails using capital letters is considered impolite — it is seen as an indication that the writer is shouting. And so on.

One can of course get by without feeling obliged to make use of these techniques, but it helps to understand the tone of the messages one receives. The e-mail has its place but is no substitute for a conventional letter, written with pen on paper and delivered by a postman.

The e-mail uses the internet to find its way to its destination. Imagine hundreds of computers all linked together and able to pass messages on to each other. The internet also supports an information service which in theory allows you to find out about practically any topic you can think of and, if you are inclined, to contribute to academic discussion! If you have an inquiring mind you will probably have already discovered the World Wide Web. Anyone who listens to the radio or who watches television will be familiar with www.co.uk and other similar abbreviations. And no one wants to get left behind!

Undoubtedly, among all the information out there, there are some useful services once you have learned how to find them. You can quite easily look up train times, go shopping, thumb through the yellow pages and even check your credit card balance at three o'clock in the morning. There are on-line discussion groups on almost any topic you can suggest. Many people have gained from finding others with specific problems and being able to share their experiences.

One aspect of internet communication is that you can remain fairly anonymous. The system is a great leveller in this respect because differences such as age are just not revealed unless you choose to reveal them. Like the telephone and the television, the internet can improve your communication with the outside world, at a time when moving about physically may be less attractive or more difficult. On the other hand, if you are still able to travel the internet provides a way of keeping in touch. At a cybercafé you can buy not only a cup of coffee but also the use of a computer connected to the system. If you have a digital camera you can send back pictures as well as messages to your friends and relatives. But don't forget to take their e-mail addresses with you!

The internet gives you access to a fantastic amount of information, but sifting out what is useful is not easy. And when you do find the subject you want there may well be too much to take in at one go. The golden rule with computing is to keep a sense of proportion — don't gather information for the sake of it, and don't use a computer at all if common sense says that for a particular activity the old-fashioned way might, after all, be preferable.

Computers can be fun. They are not just something for secretaries to write letters on and accountants to work out your tax with. They can forge commercial links and they can also provide you with a form of entertainment, linking you up, one way or another, with friends and relatives and, if you want, the rest of the world. There are people with rowing machines in their front rooms who race each other over the internet. This may sound a bit energetic for some, but you could try the same thing with a game of chess.

Admittedly, there is still some way to go before computers are as easy to use and as common as television sets — but that day will certainly come. In the meantime there is a lot of enjoyment (and frustration) to be had from them. I just hope for your sake that you don't discover too many games like Flight Simulator which allow you to pretend you are flying round the world and seeing all the great sights without leaving your chair. Addictions of that sort can be bad for your health.

MAKING THE MOST OF IT

Pushpa Chaudhary

Mary Stott

Tony Carter

Elisabeth de Stroumillo

Mike Banks

Jean Burton

PUSHPA CHAUDHARY

Lost — and found

I always thought of England as being a good country, full of warm, friendly people, where nobody had to work hard and where there was never a shortage of anything. Everything was in plentiful supply, a land of riches, with beautiful homes, where people could live happy lives.

I arrived at Heathrow on 1 October 1964 with my two daughters, aged seven and four at the time. My husband had already been in England for four years and had at last managed to save up enough money to pay for our travel. Of course, I had known about England before I arrived. I was born in Lyallpur, which is now in Pakistan, and could remember the days of British rule.

In 1947 my family had been forced to flee because we were Hindus living in a predominantly Muslim area. We settled in Jullundur, on the Punjab side of India. I was fourteen at the time of partition, and we lost everything. I can remember friends being killed and kidnapped and the mass killings that followed partition. We lived in a refugee camp for a while, and even now, at night, I sometimes dream of bloody scenes that I saw, people being butchered in their dozens and bodies piled on the streets. I don't think I will ever forget partition.

Though the bloody dismemberment of my country was caused by the British, we never felt bitter against this country. That's because we always thought of it as a place that could one day provide us with a good life and a home.

After arriving in England, what I remember most is the cold and my inability to communicate. I could not speak English at the time and it was very difficult for me to adjust to our new life. My husband and I had enjoyed quite a good standard of living in Punjab. We had our two daughters, a nice house with a beautiful mango tree in a large garden and my family lived less than twenty minutes away. I would often cycle there, visiting my brothers and sisters.

It was a comfortable life, but I suppose we had come to England for something better. There were four of us in two rooms in a house in Southall, west London. At that time the Indians, and particularly the Punjabis who were arriving in Britain, headed to Southall. There was already a small community there, so my husband settled in an area where he was surrounded by fellow countrymen. This was a strange land to us at first, but it made sense to be surrounded by people one knew.

I would often plead with my husband to go home. Life was very hard then, and I sometimes look back on it and wonder how I managed. I had two young daughters, I couldn't speak any English and I was pregnant. In total, there were fifteen people living in the house. It was hard to find accommodation in those days. It was a time when people generally just didn't want to rent out rooms to Indians, so a handful of Indians who owned their own homes rented out the rooms to those who had just arrived.

The woman who ran the house was very strict. She had been in the country a bit longer than I had, spoke some English but was not very nice to the other women in the house who did not. Hot water was only available once a week, the one time I could wash clothes. All we had were two little rooms, and it was very hard for my daughters. They were used to the freedom of our house in India, playing in a large garden with cousins and neighbours. Now we were in a cold country, stuck in two rooms. They spoke no English and for the first six months in England they didn't go to school.

I remember crying a lot, thinking of my family and just dreaming of returning to India. I never wanted to make England my home and neither did my husband. Our plan all along was to stay a few years, save money and buy land in Punjab. We were never poor there, but I suppose we just wanted more to have a really good standard of living. It's hard to earn a decent salary in India and save it, but you could do that in England because there was plenty of work. Of course, I did not go out to work

— my husband would not allow it. I was happy to stay at home and look after the family.

The first year was the hardest. After that things began to improve a little. My husband, who started work in a bakery when he first came to England, had a better job by the time my son was born in 1965. He was an educated man, unlike many friends who had come to England with him, and managed to find work as an airline booking clerk. It was quite a good job for those days.

The community in Southall in the mid-1960s was fairly small. I can remember only about two Indian shops, and finding vegetables, garlic or ginger was very difficult. People in the community all knew each other and the women would spend a lot of time visiting each other's houses. There was a lot of goodwill and camaraderie, people willing to help each other because we were all in the same boat. We all came from the same part of India, sometimes from the same towns and villages.

When we bought our first flat, all my husband's friends got together and contributed towards the deposit on it. That's how people used to buy homes in those days. My husband did the same when a friend of his wanted to buy somewhere to live. We moved into a two-bedroom flat which was not particularly large, but I was a lot happier there. I had my own place at last, a bit of privacy. I could wash and cook whenever I wanted to, and for the first time I felt much better about being in England.

I suppose the biggest problem I faced was my lack of English. It is very difficult being in a country where you are not able to communicate. But England continued to shock me. I never quite expected it to be such an unfriendly, hostile place. In the early years we witnessed and suffered quite a lot of racism, particularly once we started going out and about. I can remember gangs of white youths abusing me, but to be honest I never understood what they were saying so it didn't make much difference. At other times they would throw stones at our windows or shout abuse as they went past our house. Generally, we would just remain quiet and ignore the racism. It was not that we tolerated it, but we simply wanted to get on with our lives, work hard and get back to India as quickly as possible. I had never imagined English people could be like that.

Our children had it the hardest, but they did something we never did — they fought back. I remain very proud of their fight and, even though I am now sixty-six years old, I believe the only way to tackle racism is to fight it head on. That's what my daughters had to do, and that's what all the younger generations of Asians have done. They never put up with it like we did, and they are a credit to their community.

I remember one incident in particular. A white girl who lived near us was constantly abusing me and my daughters. Sometimes she would throw stones at our house and run away. We would call the police, but they would never come, saying it was children and they couldn't do anything. One day my eldest daughter got so angry she went out and beat the white girl up. The white girl's family called the police, and I couldn't quite believe it when the police came round to investigate. They never did the same when we were attacked! Anyhow, the point of this story is that the white girl never bothered us again. And that's what all the youngsters in Southall did — they never tolerated any racist nonsense. They learned quickly, unlike some of us.

Over the years I became used to England. My children began attending school, and by the mid-1970s there was a very large Asian community in Southall. We soon had many shops, lots of our neighbours were Asian, and the community was very strong. I can still remember many incidents involving the National Front and the police. There was lots of trouble, but we all stood together. It reminded me a bit of the freedom struggle in India. We were united and were fighting for a good cause.

Over the years I began to learn English, and this came in very useful when my husband died in 1977. For the first time in my life I had to go out to work. It was a bit difficult at first since I had only ever been used to looking after the family, and coming to terms with the bereavement was very difficult.

I had a number of jobs over the years — working in a canteen, a shop, a playgroup and a school. I didn't have much time to sit back and mourn. The most important thing was supporting the family and getting my children educated. My husband placed a lot of emphasis on education, and he would continually tell the children how important it was to make the most of the benefits of this country and study hard.

I am very proud of my children and of Asian youngsters here in general. They have worked very hard and have been a credit to their community. We didn't know much about the education system or how things worked in this country. Most of my generation either couldn't speak English or were too busy working. All I could do was provide my children with love, support and guidance, but they have done it all by themselves and have had to overcome many obstacles.

When I look back on my life I sometimes can't quite believe that England is my home, particularly as the place I came from is so far away and so different from this country. I have spent the best years of my life here, and now it feels strange for me when I go back to India. I did not keep in touch with many friends, and some of them have died. Over the years I have come to appreciate England, despite the problems we have had.

I still feel Indian, and that will never die within me, but I think of England as my home. All my immediate family are here and I have six grandchildren who live very close to me. I see them almost every day. Women also have fewer rights in India and it is much harder for them to be independent than it is here. I like the freedom I can have in England and the respect for the individual, particularly women.

I have a lot of friends here, and we have created a little India for ourselves within Britain. Southall has a very large Indian community, perhaps the biggest outside India, and at times you do not even realize you are in England. That's not such a bad thing — it's very important for older people like me, because it provides us with a lot of support and comfort. Even though I now speak English, I still sometimes have difficulty communicating. I can never express myself the way I can in my native Punjabi.

I have a part-time job in a school, looking after children at lunch-time, and I spend the rest of my spare time in the temple in Southall. Religion is very important to me, but it is also a social thing. For us the temple is like an old people's social centre. It is somewhere to go for a chat, for food and to spend time with friends. Most Asian women of my age do not like activities such as bingo, and none of us have ever drunk or smoked. We need different activities from our white counterparts, and that is why the temples are so important to us. When I go there in the afternoon it is usually very busy with older Asian women like myself.

I meditate every morning and often visit people's homes for religious ceremonies where I read the *Gita*, the Hindu holy book. The most important thing in my life now is my family and focusing on my soul for what will eventually come in the next life. Since I am a Hindu I believe in reincarnation and in attempting to find inner peace and to be at one with the universe. That is very important to me and to most Asian women when they get to my age. I have always been a vegetarian.

I have few worldly possessions. My son is responsible for running the house and takes care of all my material needs. I look after my grandchildren when they finish school. I am very content when I look back on my life. I have lived through a lot of hardships, not only in England but also during partition. But overall I think it was a good move coming to this country.

I don't think I'll ever return to India to live. I like visiting relatives, but however much I love my mother country it becomes difficult to live there when you have been away for so long. When I look at the younger generation of Asians in this country I am very proud of them. Obviously, things have changed and they are more Westernized than we have ever been. But many have tried to maintain our good traditions and have combined them with the good traditions of the West. Some people of my generation find it difficult to accept change, but that is a natural consequence of moving to a totally different country with a totally different culture.

I think change has been good for me, and I have changed enormously during the years I have been in this country. I have learned to become more independent (which I could never have done in India) and have seen the community as a whole change.

197

So what am I? How would I define my nationality or myself? This is not about the passport I carry or where I was born. I am a human being, and I believe in the oneness of all people. That is what religion has taught me. But I have also seen at close quarters how cruel people can be to each other.

MARY STOTT

Triumphs of the will

Now well into my nineties, I feel that my way of life differs very little from the life of a male nonagenarian. I live on my own, I have local social services help with washing and dressing, and I have a cooked lunch delivered to my door. I have now no "feminine" hobbies. It is quite a long while since I gave up knitting, and I never was much of a needlewoman or an embroiderer. For a number of years I have been playing piano duets . . . two-piano duets because I inherited not only my mother's precious Steinweg but a quite good piano given to my husband by a friend who retired to live in the country.

Most of the duets my friend and I play are what I used to play with my mother — Schubert, Schumann, Grieg, Beethoven. Not Bach because, for my mother, Bach's compositions were just "mental arithmetic"! Just two or three times in recent years I have been able to play a Beethoven septet arranged for four people on two pianos. Lovely fun!

Music has been an important part of my of my life ever since I was quite a young child, especially singing. It is a long time since I sang solos, even to myself, but I have been able to continue singing in a local choral society. When I was at school I remember singing alto on my own in the morning hymn, though my voice was more mezzo-soprano than contralto. I have always preferred to sing harmony rather than the melody — more interesting!

When I moved into my eighties I felt my voice was giving out on me. But, suddenly, I thought: I have a very low speaking voice. Surely these tones must be in my singing voice? So I went, a little nervously, to the conductor of a small local choir and asked him if I might join the basses. He said I was welcome and, though at first the basses thought it was rather comic having a female among them, they came to appreciate the fact that I am rather good at reading music, since I have been doing it most of my long life.

My other hobbies are gardening and painting. I have not the physical strength to do much in the garden now, but I can sow a row or two of broad beans and runner beans and seldom walk down the garden without pulling up a weed or two. I live in a house converted into four flats. We each have a rose bed and we all share the payment of a couple of gardeners, one of whom mows the lawns while the other weeds, prunes, plants and sows as he fancies.

As for my other hobby, painting, that is dwindling, alas, as I grow less mobile. But so far I have managed to go on a painting holiday every summer, and I have some wonderful souvenirs. The most precious of all was painted at midnight on 21 June 1969, when I was on holiday with one or two friends in Reykjavik. I took myself down to the beach and sat there with my paintbox as the sun went down — and immediately began to rise again.

Good as it is to have such enjoyable hobbies, they can hardly fill up the whole of one's life. What we women have to accept, I think, is that far more of us than of our male friends and relations will survive into widowhood. I think we should take this on board from the time of our retirement and involve ourselves in organizations which can provide friends as well as useful occupations. One such organization comes to mind, and that is the excellent one called the National Association of Widows.

I think, however, that our daughters are less likely to survive into a lonely old age than we were. The pattern of society is changing. Far more women are now in full-time paid employment, and far more husbands and sons involve themselves willingly in family and home. I myself am truly grateful for the fact that my two grandsons-in-law are both very good "househusbands". My two little great-granddaughters have been able to rely upon Daddy not only to take them for walks but also to prepare the milk bottle for the younger one to suck.

Alas for me, when my daughter, my only child, was born my husband was in the Navy. He sailed off in a minesweeper to the Mediterranean when she was only a fortnight old, and we did not see him for two long years. But we managed. My parents-in-law moved in with me, and I went back to work part-time to earn money to keep the household going.

I was lucky in my profession. Sex prejudice has never, I think, been rampant in the journalistic world — though it did hit me now and then. If I had been a man I should almost certainly have become editor of the *Co-operative News* in Manchester when the then editor left us. If I had been a man I should probably have become deputy chief sub-editor of the *Manchester Evening News* where I worked happily at the end of the war when most of the male staff were still in the Forces. But, explaining why I was not allowed to take charge on Saturdays when the chief sub had his day off, the editor said: "We have to safeguard the succession, Mary, and the successor has to be a man."

To me it seems obvious that putting thoughts, observations and opinions into words cannot be categorized as a male or a female skill, and that applies also to quite a few other occupations. Now we have a female monarch, we have had a female Prime Minister, and we have had a female Speaker of the House of Commons. So may we not be pretty confident that change will come? And we women should remember that women tend to live longer than men, so we shall have more years in which to get training for top jobs. I do believe that in the twenty-first century women will walk hand in hand with men, as level partners.

TONY CARTER

Making oneself heard

Do older people need a voice? Do they have interests apart from the rest of the population? Even if they have, don't the usual political parties and interest groups represent those interests? After all, older people demonstrate their competence every day of the week — no constituency party of any persuasion is without its quota of energetic older volunteers. To a considerable extent, retired people run the local groups of the National Trust, the Royal Society for the Protection of Birds, the Women's Institute, the Townswomen's Guild and a dozen others. They are the backbone of meals on wheels and other services. Surely they can make their voices heard.

Yes, but . . .

A town centre street is to be pedestrianized. Wonderful! A traffic-free zone. No buses. Children can play. The young bloods can rollerblade at will, weaving in and out, scaring the old folk. But did anyone ask frailer older people if they could manage to walk down the precinct, do their shopping, walk back with a heavy bag? Before, they could hop on a bus for a couple of stops. Pensioners now get a fuel allowance of £100 (well, some do — the small print is more complicated). Perhaps they might have preferred a couple of pounds on their weekly pension. Were they asked?

It is not just government, local or national, that ignores the possibility of there being a specific "older" view. Security cameras have been installed on the high street; civil liberty groups are outraged and civic amenity groups protest. Did anyone ask if older people might feel safer venturing out when the cameras were working?

At sixty, having been retired from full-time work three years, I got a job. It was as coordinator of a campaign on health in old age. The job involved running events putting forward a positive view of view of health in later life and encouraging community health activities. I knew nothing about health but did not have to; my job was really an organizer or what, quickly picking up the jargon of the voluntary sector, I learned to call a facilitator. One day I visited a group of pensioners who had expressed interest in the work of the campaign. To get the discussion going I asked what they saw as the major health issue for older people in their town. The reply was: "Transport."

What they meant of course was that inadequate transport made it difficult to get to the swimming baths, the park, a local mutual education project or indeed anywhere that provided opportunities for stimulating, healthy or outdoor activity. At another level, they undoubtedly had a sense that poor transport contributed towards the isolation of older people, that it restricted social life and the ability to enjoy the town's facilities and that a poorer lifestyle could lead to the earlier onset of dependency.

The episode taught me something about health but also drew my attention to the connection between things. It was not enough to press for a session at the local swimming baths specifically for older people — it was necessary also to check on local transport facilities. We now have a new bit of jargon for this kind of reasoning; it is called "joined-up thinking".

That should not really have been a surprise to me. Most of my working life had been spent in the trade union movement. A trade union officer does not spend the whole time working on the next pay increase for the members; most of the time is spent worrying about a vast range of other matters. These might be related to health and safety, welfare, promotion opportunities, training opportunities, procedural matters like a discipline code, holiday arrangements — even the well-being and profitability of the employer. These are important and interrelated issues and go towards a worker feeling he has a stake in his job which is more than the pay packet.

Not long after the discussion with the pensioners described above I met an old trade union friend who told me he was chair of Greater London

Forum for the Elderly. This was my introduction to senior citizens' forums — locally based alliances of older people and the organizations to which they belong or who are concerned about them. Having discovered such bodies, my colleague in the health campaign and I adopted them as a useful base, where they existed, for local health action. We were impressed by the ways that older people had discovered of making known their views to local authorities and other local bodies. When our two-year contract finished we sought and obtained funding to undertake a study of how older people and their organizations influence local policy-making.

Forums had been in existence since the early 1980s but were by no means the first attempt to give a voice to the aspirations of older people. In his excellent book *No Thanks to Lloyd George* (published by Third Age Press), Dave Goodman recounts the early history of the prolonged struggle for the old age pension, involving a wide range of political, social and religious groups as well as philanthropic individuals. Isolated groupings of pensioners carried on campaigning and representing older people, leading in the early 1940s to the first national organization, the National Federation of Old Age Pensioners (now usually known as Pensioners' Voice). Retired workers in some large employers, such as the Civil Service and the Post Office but also outside the public sector, formed retirement associations, which in some cases became independent and powerful organizations.

In the 1970s and 1980s some trade unions, led by the Transport and General Workers' Union, formed associations for their retired members. These, like the employer-based associations, provided continuing opportunities for keeping up the contacts and fellowship of working life but also became campaigning organizations, notably on issues concerning the state retirement pension. This period also saw the establishment of the Association of Retired Persons (later, following merger with another group, adding Over 50) in deliberate imitation of the successful mass-membership lobbying organization of that name in the USA. It has become an effective lobbying organization and offers a range of benefits appealing mainly to middle-class pensioners but has not as yet achieved the very substantial membership of its American model.

Meanwhile the National Pensioners' Convention was formed to bring together all existing organizations of retired and older people in order to present a common view, in particular to the government. After a number of problems it is now well established, with an office and paid staff, is increasingly consulted by the voluntary sector and has established a dialogue with the government. It is an umbrella organization for most of the large national groupings of retired and older people and so has to work by consensus, mainly on issues where there is overwhelming agreement on the objective. The obvious example is state pension provision, though even on this issue there have been quite sharp differences of emphasis between member organizations.

More recently it has begun to demonstrate an interest in other issues of concern to older people and has been encouraged to do so, partly by older people themselves but also by the voluntary sector. Increasingly, the part of the voluntary sector concerned primarily with older people has attempted to draw into discussion representatives of older people themselves. Age Concern England and Help the Aged, in their policy formation work, have led this move, but others have taken the hint. So, for instance, the report of the Royal Commission on Long Term Care, called *With Respect to Old Age,* led to some sharply expressed urging of government action on the part of the voluntary sector, in which the National Pensioners' Convention joined.

Changing attitudes on the part of the government and the voluntary sector demonstrate an awareness, not only of the increasingly representative character of the NPC but also of the need for an independent voice speaking for older people. No one, least of all the organized pensioners' movement, underestimates the essential role of the great voluntary sector organizations, both in service provision and in applying resources to working out or commenting upon policies for older people. This essential work needs to be reinforced and confirmed by the views of older people themselves, and in this the organizations of older people can play an important role.

This brings us back to the local scene. It is here that vital decisions of concern to older people are made on health and care. The power which the local authority and the health authority (and, now, primary care groups) have to affect and reshape the life of older people far exceeds their powers over any other section of the population, except children. The comparison may be telling; many older people complain of being treated like children.

The health authority can decide whether or not they stay in hospital, how long they have to wait for treatment (and there is plenty of evidence collected, among others, by Age Concern and the Association of Retired Persons Over 50, suggesting that older people are discriminated against in these respects). The local authority can decide if the older person needs help at home, what sort of help that is to be and for what periods and how much it will cost. Though there is a statutory duty to provide these facilities, standards of care — and of charging — are vague. As a result, standards and charges vary widely. In theory the person concerned and his or her relatives are supposed to be consulted, but often they feel timid or overawed by officialdom.

A particularly useful way of expressing local opinion on behalf of older people is through the senior citizens' forums. These started to develop in London and the Strathclyde region of Scotland in the early 1980s. Slowly at first, but with increasing momentum, forums spread throughout the country.

Though some forums are membership based, they will typically bring together all the local organizations concerned with older people. These might be of pensioners, such as the local branch of the British Pensioners' and Trade Union Action Association or Pensioners' Voice, organizations concerned directly with older people, such as the Age Concern group, or those with a more general interest in older people, like the churches. All these come together to decide on a common approach to a matter of local concern. They do not restrict themselves to care issues.

In such ways the views of Britain's older people are gradually making themselves heard. Encouragement has been at hand through the Cabinet Office's "Better Government for Older People" programme which has been addressing some of the issues of closer involvement of older people in government through a programme of pilot projects and information. These first years of the new millennium will see some significant steps in establishing a voice for older people in Britain.

ELISABETH DE STROUMILLO

With and without a stick

Travel has played a major part in my life since the age of nine months when my mother took me to India to join my father on a tea plantation. I can't pretend to remember anything about that six-week sea voyage, but I do recall most vividly a host of other childhood journeys, both within India and, for the regular "leaves" planters got every four years, back to Europe for several months' meandering between friends, relations and pleasurable or cultural high-spots in Italy, France, England and Wales.

The nomadic existence obviously suited me because, later, travel became for forty years not only the linchpin of my working life but also my chief holiday objective. Working or playing, with or without family, alone or in groups, I've done it all ways; and now that I'm well past the official retirement post the only thing that puts a brake on the wandering (apart from a comparatively recent passion for my garden and my grandchildren) is lack of limitless cash to fund it.

Admittedly I'm lucky, blessed with pretty robust health and a still lively curiosity about places familiar and unknown and their people, and as long as nothing changes much in those two departments I cannot see any significant difference between my enjoyment of travel before and after the age of sixty. Nor can I understand why people insist on making such a distinction; the only time I've ever been rendered almost speechless with fury was when some daft television presenter opened a programme aimed at senior travellers by asking me what sort of holidays were "suitable" for them. "Any and all they really want to take, and feel up to taking" is the short answer I didn't make so pithily at the time.

I was born too early to experience what my own young and their more affluent contemporaries considered part of their education: the "year off" spent humping a backpack round the world. Air travel when I was in my late teens was prohibitively expensive and the notion of lowering fares to fill otherwise empty seats and increase profitability was still to be born. Airlines were all government-owned, after all, and competition was controlled by a world-wide regulatory body that even determined the size of on-board meals and the price of alcoholic drinks.

But a few years later, when the advent of charter flight began to shake up the travel industry, I did a more modest form of travelling rough. Cheap night-flights to Greece, for example, followed by many long and bumpy bus rides, bedding down either on hard mattresses in private houses or in a sleeping bag unrolled on equally uncomfortable beaches was not only rewarding in its own right but also vastly preferable to not visiting Greece at all.

Perhaps I wouldn't find that sort of thing quite so amusing today as I once did. As the years roll by, one does rate rather more highly the private bathroom, at least, however basic it may be. (I've known some pretty basic ones, too, including one where that first much-needed wash in the hand-basin instantly drenched my still-shod feet because it lacked both plug and waste pipe.) It's equally true that the freedom a hired car affords is more desirable than being tied to bus schedules, usually at unsociable hours. But if the goal was irresistible and other options non-existent, I dare say I'd give it a go.

As I see it, therefore, the main difference between travelling before and after that age watershed is the likelihood of having by sixty-plus lost, for one reason or another, your nearest and dearest fellow travellers. You may have been widowed or have a spouse who no longer wants or feels able to go away. I've had umpteen plaintive letters from older people whose other halves refuse to put the dog or cat into kennels even for a fortnight's break.

Your children are tied to their jobs and their own families, or the cousin/best friend you've always gone with is suddenly incapacitated for the foreseeable future, so it's decision time. Do you go completely solo, or with a possibly randomly chosen companion, or do you opt for a group package? One outfit that has made a success over the years in "matching" solo travellers who need company but don't know anyone suitable is Solo Holidays, which can be reached on 020 8951 2800.

Temperament plays the most important part in making this choice. For anyone plagued by loneliness, who becomes terminally depressed without a companion more or less permanently on hand to exchange opinions and impressions with, even to the extent of sharing bedrooms (I know that budgetary considerations can also make this necessary), then going solo is out of the question.

If on the other hand, like me, you're far from reclusive but still rather enjoy your own company; if you don't need to share a room for the sake of economy and positively relish spells of being alone without having to make allowances for anyone else's likes, dislikes and idiosyncrasies, then you can dismiss the second option. Here I must add that I have, when it was unavoidable, cheerfully shared rooms with highly incompatible people, most memorably with Doris in Beijing, where single rooms were rare at the time.

Doris didn't smoke; I did — in the corridor or in the lounge where, each evening, I made notes on the day's events while she washed out her corsets and went early to bed. Retiring much later, I had to steer, in the dark, around the dripping underwear strung across both bathroom and bedroom, but on days when we didn't have an early start I reckoned I could at least look forward to a bit of extra sleep in the morning. Not a bit of it: Doris always woke at her usual ghastly hour and, despite my anguished growls of refusal, would reach for the insulated bedside flask of boiled water and trill out an offer of tea. Despite all that, we became quite fond of one another.

Even if you don't need or want to share a room, there still remains the question of whether to go solo or join a group, and that depends as much as anything on the sort of trip you're contemplating. If I know a country well, and speak the language adequately, I would always choose to go on my own, tailoring my itinerary to avoid giving myself too much ground to cover in any one day if I'm driving. Punctures and such minor mishaps I can cope with (a helpful knight invariably chances along eventually, even in the remotest places). I can even bear to do without lunch if wayside pit-stops are absent; over-tiredness is the only unbeatable enemy.

Having reached the chosen hotel and settled in, the moment most lone travellers dread above all is the one where they have to venture into the bar or dining-room unescorted. I eliminate the bar problem by carrying my own tipple and refreshing myself in the privacy of my room. The only occasion I varied this routine was in Moscow, long before the Iron Curtain went up, when I was writing for a national newspaper whose readers, I reckoned, might want to know about Soviet hotel bars.

It was a seriously depressing experiment. Not wanting to look silly by asking for whisky, I requested a Bloody Mary (vodka with tomato juice). "No Bloody Mary. Screwdriver," barked the surly barmaid. What on earth was a Screwdriver, I wondered. "Vodka and orange," she snapped. Could I just have vodka on the rocks, then? "No vodka on rocks. Screwdriver," she almost bellowed, so I had a Screwdriver. The orange juice content, as I'd feared, was foul.

The dining-room dilemma is also easily solved: never, ever appear in one without a book, holding it — if you're a woman — prominently to indicate that you are deeply sincere and pose no threat to innocent and vulnerable males who might also be dining alone. A friend insists that a crossword puzzle is a simpler shield against curious glances and consequent embarrassment because it doesn't entail having to turn pages, admittedly a bit tricky while eating. I've tried a crossword but felt rather foolish when I was stumped over a clue and had to gaze into space while thinking about it, so I shall stick to books. A heavy room-key can at least prevent the pages from turning themselves.

The lone woman shouldn't insulate herself against strangers all the time, though, unless she's happy to forgo the pleasures of surprising chance encounters. I would never have met Phyllis B. Popkin if I hadn't been alone and, though there can't be many like her around, there are many others only slightly less exotic. We came across one another in the USA, at an "historic" inn in Virginia (eighteenth-century fare prepared by costumed wenches) where I'd gone for lunch after visiting Monticello, the amazing home that America's third President, Thomas Jefferson, created for himself.

Having collected some food, I took my tray on to the broad balcony and sat at a half-empty table. Opposite me sat a beatifically beaming woman who had clearly finished eating but was equally clearly waiting for something. It turned out to be me. She opened the conversation by remarking that she lived near by, often ate there and would normally have gone home much earlier. Keen intuition, however, told her to stay on for a meaningful experience.

She passed me her card which, beneath her name, read: "Happiness Consultant/For greater awareness of the Divine Love, Joy and Assistance that is always available to us ..." She wasn't merely a hallelujah-merchant, it turned out, though she professed to be able to contact "People and Pets Who've Passed On" if that's what you wanted. For "People Living on Earth" she also produced "Laughter Products and Programs" (squeaky cushions? I didn't dare ask), "Seminars on Trusting Intuition" and books such as *Have You Seen Any Good Miracles Lately*?

She expounded a bit about her intuition, which did not only function over trivial matters like making her await my arrival but had also saved many people from disastrous mistakes that might have ruined their lives. She wasn't touting for business, I'm sure: she was very sweet and she could recognize from the start that I was a bird of passage. Reluctant to prove a total let-down, I dredged the backwaters of my mind for a meaningful titbit and came up with a grandmother who had a not unfounded reputation for occasionally predicting the future. I only hope she found it meaningful enough.

On the question of group travel, it's the option I would go for if the other members were like-minded. I've enjoyed many a working jaunt with fellow-journalists because we all shared a common purpose — to get a "story". Even if I knew no one in the party I'd still choose to join a group to pursue some special interest like history or music or horticulture: you gain so much by being with other, probably more knowledgeable, enthusiasts.

The advantages of being shepherded by a guest-lecturer are great and so, too, is erudite company. I perfectly understood the lady passenger on a highly cultural Swan Hellenic cruise who preferred sunning herself by the pool to attending lectures or going on excursions. She was there, she said, because after the sun went down there were so many amusing and intelligent fellow-passengers to mix with.

I'd also choose to go with a group to any place I was totally unfamiliar with; Syria was the most recent example in my experience. Despite a strong predilection for Middle Eastern countries, I'd only been there once, fleetingly: three nights in

Damascus with one full day at Palmyra — barely long enough to justify putting a tick against its name on the must-go list and certainly giving not the slightest inkling of how many more dizzying and often barely known riches it contains. I'd go back like a shot if anyone devised a second-time-round tour, but it's not for tackling on your own without any Arabic; though the people are lovely, I suspect there would be terrible problems making all the arrangements.

Finally, a word about two slight worries that might assail solo travellers contemplating a first group holiday, the first being that they mightn't get on with the rest of the party. Even if the proposed trip is only to escape winter weather for a week, that fear is likely to be groundless. There are always a few people you can happily pass the time of day with (and, if not, it's not too hard to put up with boredom for a week, especially if you've armed yourself with a few books).

If it's a longer trip, with a serious purpose like learning something about Syria, then nearly everyone will be compatible — but avoid "bonding" with any one of them too quickly. The inevitable prize bore or two may well make a beeline for you, so study the field for a few days before you get stuck with them and tarred with the same brush.

Secondly — and this applies mainly to the "serious" type of trip — will you be able to keep up if everyone else is younger and more active? Answer: yes, if you take a walking-stick with you or, better still, one that doubles as a perch; in my politically incorrect youth it was called a shooting-stick. It identifies you as someone to slow down a bit for, not least in the eyes of whoever's in charge; no shame in that. You may well — in fact most certainly do — have a lot more stamina than many younger members of the party (this is especially true of the eighty-plus age group, I've found), but that is absolutely *no* reason not to play the age card. When you're dealt it, play it.

MIKE BANKS

Old men of Hoy

The Old Man of Hoy is one of Britain's northernmost sentinels, thrust out into the grey Atlantic from the desolate, rock-bound coast of the Orkney island of Hoy. In a supremely melodramatic gesture, this slender rock pillar stabs 450 feet into the sky like the admonishing finger of some titanic Nordic god. Composed of layered sandstone, the soaring column is cut away on every side by the relentless pounding of the ocean. Predictably it has now become a myth in the climbing world, and every year a trickle of young men and women made the long pilgrimage into the north to test their strength and resolution against the disdainful giant.

Old men have dreams. In 1990, at the age of sixty-seven, I wondered if I might possibly manage to climb the Old Man. I would thereby reassure myself that, both physically and mentally, I was still clinging on. If I made it, I would be the oldest climber ever to do so. I had been rock-climbing and mountaineering since my mid-twenties so I had a realistic idea of what I would be letting myself in for.

The idea gnawed away at me. Then a young(ish) climbing friend, Colin Beechey (then forty-one), casually mentioned that he yearned to have a go. The game was on. I put in a month's training, with daily sessions on my garden wall to strengthen my fingers interspersed with cliff climbs in Cornwall.

Things began to look good when *Saga Magazine* agreed to sponsor the project and engaged John Cleare, a mountain photographer, to record our ascent. The idea was that, as Colin and I climbed, John would get close-ups by moving up beside us using sliding clamps to ascend a fixed rope. He would be swinging in space like a spider, and it seemed to me a pretty desperate way of earning a living! To complete the picture, Geoff Axbey came along to take photographs from the clifftop.

Plane, ferry and taxi eventually deposited us at Rackwick Bay on Hoy, and straight away we set off on the hour's walk to take a look at the Old Man himself. To get to sea level a descending traverse led down 400 feet across a worryingly steep grassy cliffside. The lower we got the more the Old Man towered above us, overhang stacked on overhang. Then it started to drizzle, making the prospect even more intimidating. We trudged home in silence, each of us plagued by his personal doubts and fears. Later we all confessed that we slept fitfully that night.

Next morning the weather was brighter and so were we. At the foot of the climb we roped up. Colin led up the first 90 feet of steep but relatively easy rock to a wide ledge. John and I followed, warming up nicely for the struggle which we knew would now ensue.

The next pitch of 120 feet was the *pièce de résistance* of the whole climb. It would start with a tricky sideways traverse of about 30 feet. This would land us under some fearsome overhangs which would have to be climbed. All this would take place over a sheer drop of 200 feet into the sea.

Colin started across the traverse. Halfway he had to step across a gap with miserably inadequate handholds while at the same time he was forced outwards by a bulge in the rock. "God, this is hard," he muttered. A few tense moves and he was across. He then climbed a vertical wall to the first overhang, moved out right and disappeared above out of sight. I could only gauge his progress by the rate at which I paid out the rope. After a long while — or so it seemed to me — the rope was hauled in tight.

My turn now! The sea crashed far below and the adrenaline started to pump. I edged along the ledge until I came to a full stop at the hard step. The obvious ledge above my head was rounded and covered with slippery grit. No use at all. I located a small vertical hold for my left hand. Reaching across I came across a concealed finger hold for my right.

224

Teetering on the edge of balance I delicately eased across, and all was well.

Looking up for the first time, I saw the first of the great overhangs jutting out above me. I climbed up the vertical back wall until I was below the overhanging roof. The trick then was to haul out on to the right wall, work up and under the overhang and finally squirm round its right-hand side. I was delighted when these moves turned out well and I found myself climbing in balance again above the overhang.

So far so good, but I knew the real brute of an overhang was the next one. I climbed up an enclosed crack, about as wide as a coffin, until my head bumped against the roof of the overhang. This jutted out 4 feet into space and the walls of the crack were smooth except for two small footholds. How on earth was I expected to reach 4 feet back into space, grab hold of nothing and hoist myself out of this one? This was the scariest move of the whole climb.

Arching backwards I could just grasp the loop of a nylon sling Colin had placed. I heaved on it, got my foot on to the vital hold on the left. Another heave. Up with the right leg on to the other foothold. One final heave and I was there, panting and elated. The crack above was smooth and vertical, even overhanging at one spot. But I could see Colin's smiling face and I muscled my way up this relentless crack to arrive on a small ledge and congratulate Colin on his bold lead.

John now followed. Climbing the rope on his clamps, swinging out over space, gently rotating. Soon all three of us were huddled on the ledge, delighted that the hardest part was below us. Colin led two long pitches, wending his way between overhangs, up cracks and across bulging walls. Finally there was an awesome-looking corner, like an open book with a crack at the back, which soared up the summit. It turned out to be the most enjoyable pitch of the whole climb. Superbly steep but amply provided with lovely sharp little holds, it was a rock-climber's delight and a fitting climax. Then we were all on the top, waving to Geoff who was photographing us from the clifftop opposite. I had the added thrill of having achieved the age record of sixty-seven for the ascent.

However, we were far from relaxed. We had a really hairy descent before us. At the top of each pitch we would thread a doubled rope through a sling tied to the rock and lower ourselves down. Climbers call this abseiling. However, on the bottom pitch below the overhangs we would be left swinging some 20 feet out in space. Our rope would stop 200 feet above the sea and it was then vital that somehow we haul ourselves back into the rock to land on a small ledge. To achieve this we had left a spare rope tied in place, top and bottom.

John was first down. We saw him pass the lower overhang and swing out in space. Then he disappeared from sight. Then it was Colin's turn. Though he was our star climber who had led the

226

route with such skill and courage, he was petrified at the prospect of this abseil. Once launched he made it in good style, as I knew he would.

My turn came and I gulped as I looked down to the sea below. At last I was below the overhangs, swinging clear in space, looking down to the upturned faces of Colin and John. I lowered away until John shouted: "Smile, please." My grin, I suspect, was fraught and fleeting!

So it ended with the elation of fulfilment and the warmth of comradeship which makes climbing such a great game. Back home I got on with life, taking time off whenever possible to go climbing. Four years had rolled by when my friend, Richard Sykes, had a brainwave. He had formed a charity in Bristol called Westcare whose aim was to bring support and hope to sufferers of that little-understood but potentially devastating disease ME or chronic fatigue syndrome. Richard suggested that we repeat the Old Man of Hoy as a fundraising charity climb. In passing, I would also push the age record up to seventy-one.

In September 1994 it all came together. This time we had television cameraman Jim Curran with us: "Big Jim", a laughing, adventurous man with a nice sense of humour. He took one look at me and blurted out: "Good Lord, you are seriously old!"

Our return visit to the Old Man was notable for two reasons: we hit the height of the midge season, those ferocious biting insects which are Scotland's answer to the mosquito. Jim Curran and my wife, who were photographing on the clifftop, were driven to near distraction. As we climbed the landward face, a violent thunderstorm was rolling in from the sea. We only became aware of it with the crash of thunder.

The climb was led by the then sixty-one-year-old Richard. He continued, despite the downpour, slowly surmounting the wet and slippery vertical rock. It would have been a sterling effort for a young man. For an oldie it was positively heroic. As we reached the summit the clouds drew back to give us a glorious sunset followed by a hasty retreat down the ropes. We had raised some £16,000 for the charity and I had pushed the age record up to seventy-one.

But records are made to be broken. The following year a Manchester man, Ron Whitehead, climbed it at the age of seventy-six. A splendid effort. However, when I became seventy-six I got in touch with Ron only to hear the riveting news that he intended to climb it in 2000 when he would be eighty! I wished him the best of luck.

Certainly at seventy-seven I still enjoy mountaineering. Sometimes I am asked what my dark secret is. I am seldom able to come up with a convincing reply. I have always led an active life, mentally and physically, including a career of twenty-seven years in the Royal Marine Commandos. I have never smoked, but I love a glass or two of wine — in moderation. For the last forty years my wife and I have kept to a vegetarian diet of nutritious, non-fatty, organic food. My climbing keeps me fit and sharpens me up mentally. But all this does not quite explain why I have not eased up. I think the only honest answer is that, up to now, that thought has not even occurred to me. It really is all in the mind.

JEAN BURTON

The blue yonder

Then I saw there was a Way to Hell — even from the Gates of Heaven.

> — John Bunyan,
> *Pilgrim's Progress*

Perhaps you have been discussing retirement for years. Very possibly it has been a cosy pipe dream that has kept your sanity intact when you have been stuck in traffic jams, when the demands of work and family have driven you to distraction or when you have seen yet another weather forecast predicting poor air quality in your area whereas in the South-West the sun sign has beckoned invitingly.

Yes, you have said to yourself, on retirement it's a Nest in the West for you. A thatched cottage perhaps, with real roses round the door, a garden with a spot where you can sit gazing out to sea, sipping your favourite drink as you let the world wag on without you. This, you have told yourself, will be the time to meditate, to appreciate the Quality of Life, to really get away from it all.

Of course, there have been those Jeremiahs who have warned you that it would be a mistake to cut yourself off from friends and family, that you will find it lonely in a new place, that you could always take holidays and you don't have to live there. But, you have said to yourself, they're all stick-in-the-muds, old before their time. You, on the other hand, have the Spirit of Adventure. Life is What You Make It.

The children, as you have it planned, would spend their holidays with you. The grandchildren would love to play in the sand and swim in the sea. Friends would come to visit. You would, of course, keep open house — everyone welcome.

You would walk into the village and carry back your provisions in a rucksack, after a reviving drink in your adopted pub, chatting up the locals. A little fishing, perhaps, and you might even buy a boat, do some sailing. Loneliness, you have assured yourself, would never be a problem.

So, all you have to do is find a suitable place.

Out with the 4 × 4, only pausing to adjust the bull bars — there's wildlife on those moors — and you hammer down the motorways at more than 80 miles an hour. "No distance at all," you inwardly coo. You simply *know* you are doing the right thing. After Okehampton the traffic builds up perceptibly and you are reduced to a crawl. But you are nearly there. Soon there's the hotel. In more senses than one, you have arrived.

Next morning you hit the estate agents running, collecting masses of house details. You feel surprised and lucky: there seems to be an amazing selection of property on the market. Pity about that parking ticket: you didn't notice the sign banning parking in the summer. Anyway it did seem to be the only place you could leave a big car.

You select the most interesting properties from the bundles you have picked up and set off on your first tour of inspection. A shame you have left the Ordnance Survey map behind, but the road signs will guide. Soon, however, it becomes apparent that you're lost and you're facing a large tractor coming in the opposite direction. "I'm not reversing for anyone," you declare and you squeeze past, scraping the car on the Cornish hedge which, you subsequently discover, was a wall.

The farmer has shouted something at you, but you can't understand his accent — but it's quite clear he doesn't sound very friendly. Round the next bend there's a combine harvester. This time you have no choice but to reverse — only to discover that the other side of your vehicle has now been seriously scratched.

Then, eventually, you are able to tell yourself you have found it. Your Nest in the West. Not quite what you dreamed of, but it does have that elusive something called Character. Give it a new roof, some heating and a lick of paint and you've worked miracles. Anyway, the view is fantastic: nothing really between the cottage and the sea, just a few fields and farm buildings. Lovely!

The garden looks a bit of a jungle, but you'll soon hack that down. Clearly the hedges will all have to come out, but they do spoil the view. Then there's mains water and electricity to see to. But it is not even really isolated — there's a farm and there are other cottages near by and it's only two miles from the village, with a shop, a pub and a post office. It is, you say to yourself, ideal.

Two years later, however, you have become a somewhat sadder and wiser person, and the "For Sale" sign is rusting outside. Finding a builder, a plumber, an electrician has proved almost impossible, materials are scarce and delivery costs are horrendous. The doctor is unwilling to visit and the hospital is twenty miles away. The garden took a long time to clear and you now know what that hedge was for: the wind has killed off all your plants and shrubs. The grass has had to be cut once a week in winter and more frequently in the summer.

The weather has been so unexpected as to leave you speechless: the rain gets in everywhere, even through glass, and the snails eat the putty. Double-glazing has turned out to be too expensive, as you have already spent a fortune on repair jobs to the roof. The planners have refused your application for an extension, but they have passed the one for 150 caravans down the lane. These now block your lovely view and do their bit to impede access to your property.

You don't walk into the village any more, even though you've given up the Gortex and the Timberland boots for polar fleece, oilskins and wellies. The howling gales and the horizontal rain haven't helped very much, and the groceries weigh such a lot when your back is bad. The locals, it has transpired, are too busy to chat, and the few other "expats" around will only pass the time of day to talk about their problems — they have no inclination to listen to yours.

The family no longer come down to visit. It's too far away for them to come for a weekend and the grandchildren have already decided they want more exciting holidays. You've been back to visit them a number of times, but suddenly it seems no one has time for you. They have their own lives to lead, and you are out of it now.

Anyway, the children's spare rooms are too small and uncomfortable and, more to the point, you discover when you return that the burglars have visited and that the local cattle have broken through the fence. How you wish you hadn't complained about the noise and the smell of the farm.

So, with mixed feelings, you decide it's time to call it a day and you tell yourself you want to get back to civilization. But the only people remotely interested in purchasing your erstwhile dream home are a young village couple who can't afford the asking price. The realization hits you that you are going to have to sell at a loss, and this at a time when property prices in every other part of the country have rocketed.

But if none of this scenario deters you, and you are really an independent sort who likes your own company and are skilled at DIY and driving, are prepared to search your chosen area carefully, visiting in all seasons, and you are also of the opinion that your children should be able to stand on their own feet after the age of twenty-one and that they don't owe you a thing, well, why not take the plunge and make your dream a reality?

Our experience has been one of pulling up roots from near London some fifteen years ago, and we have reached a level of satisfaction where we simply wouldn't go back. Along the way we have met many kind people who have given us a helping hand and some who haven't. But we like to think — to hope — that we have learned from our mistakes.

Perhaps you wonder what we do all day. My answer, now that the house is weatherproof and the garden is tamed, is that I don't really know. The time goes by so quickly. Routine chores are often sorely neglected because there is so much else to do. We have a dog that needs to be exercised and we have other animals to care for. We like to go bird-watching and to seek out wild flowers; we enjoy visiting the seals and sometimes we see dolphins and basking sharks.

We like to watch the ships sail past: the *QEII* and other big cruise liners, and indecipherable naval vessels which bristle with electronic gadgets, cargo ships and tankers, trawlers and other fishing boats, tall ships and yachts, as well as helicopters whose pilots may be practising their skills with the lifeboat crews. It is all endlessly fascinating.

But my favourite time is when, on winter evenings, we sit around the wood-burner. I listen to the roar of the wind and the sea, as the cats purr and the dog snores. Then I know that I am content.

Summer of course brings the visitors. Some of them come every year without fail, and we know them well. We listen to their news and we inspect their latest cars. We welcome new faces, rescue them if they are lost, recommend hotels and other accommodation, suggest places to visit and, if asked, give the time of the ferry.

But, with the swallows, the visitors depart and life resumes its normal pattern. We check the roof, the windows, the fuel supplies, and we stock up on candles, torch batteries and food, and we settle down to another winter.

You may think that this is life in the slow lane, perhaps even life in the lay-by. But it is a life which suits us fine. We feel we have been successful immigrants.

About the contributors

Mike Banks was born in 1922, is an ex-Commando, polar explorer, Himalayan mountaineer and author. In 1952 – 4 he made an 800-mile crossing of the Greenland ice-cap (and was awarded the Polar Medal). In 1958 he climbed Rakaposhi, at that time the highest non-oxygen summit attained by a British climber, and was awarded the MBE.

Paulette Bauckham is a professional social worker, specializing in the care of older people. She is now a freelance consultant, presenting training programmes for staff in residential, day-care and hospital settings. Here she has drawn on the book of which she is co-author, *The Therapeutic Purposes of Reminiscence* (published by Sage).

Jean Burton was born in 1938, the daughter of a Methodist minister. She was educated at Leeds University before taking up teaching. She retired early to Cornwall where she enjoys walking her dog, reading and solving crosswords.

Tony Carter was born in 1925. He was a senior trade union official in the Post Office. On retirement he became coordinator of the Health Education Authority/Age Concern Age Well Campaign and worked with the Centre for Health and Retirement Education. Until 1999 he was chairperson of the Greater London Forum for the Elderly.

Barbara Castle, Baroness Castle of Blackburn, was born in 1910. She was a journalist before becoming an MP in 1945 and was successively Minister for Transport, Employment, Health and Social Security. She was a Euro-MP from 1979 to 1985 and has been a Labour peer since 1990. Pensions, and poetry are among her many interests.

Pushpa Chaudhary was born in Lyallpur, India (now Pakistan) in 1933 and came to England in 1964. She was a teacher before and after emigrating, and now, when she is not teaching Hindi and dancing to the children of the local Indian community, she works in the temple bookshop and as a dinner lady for the local community.

Michael Dunne, MBE, was born in 1915. He was a researcher and author with the Consumers' Association and then research manager with the Research Institute for Consumer Affairs. Recently he was a disability consultant with the RICA and is now much involved in a voluntary capacity with a number of disability agencies.

Gillian Ford was born in 1934. From 1990 to 1997 she was director of Marie Curie Cancer Care. She was previously director of studies at St Christopher's Hospice, south London, and has held various senior posts at the Department of Health, where she was Deputy Chief Medical Officer from 1977 to 1985.

Dave Goodman was born in 1915. He was a volunteer in Spain with the International Brigade. Many years later he went as a mature student to Hull University. He became a lecturer in further and adult education and then Warden of Wedgwood Memorial College, Staffordshire. He is chairperson of the North Staffordshire Pensioners' Convention and in 2000 was awarded an honorary DLitt by Staffordshire University.

Angela Graham is Scottish but was born in London in 1937. She trained as a sociologist at Leeds University and became a medical social worker, going on later to undertake an MA in Social Policy at Brunel University. She is married with two grown-up sons and a granddaughter, and she enjoys continuing education, travel, the theatre and good books.

Denis Healey, Lord Healey of Riddlesden, was born in 1917. He has been a life-long Labour activist. He was an MP from 1957 to 1992, being successively Defence Secretary, Chancellor of the Exchequer and Deputy Party Leader. He became a Labour member of the House of Lords in 1992, and he is the author of several books.

Vera Ivers was born in 1931. She left school at fourteen to train as a nurse and later became a social worker in the voluntary sector. She worked closely with the Beth Johnson Foundation and was its principal officer for development. She got an MA at sixty-four and has served on her local council. She is a member of the Cabinet Committee on Better Government for Older People and chairperson of the Older Women's Network for the UK.

Peter Laslett was born in 1915. He was a talks producer for the BBC Third Programme. A Fellow of Trinity College, Cambridge, since 1953, he was co-founder and director of the Cambridge Group for the History of Population. He was also a co-founder of the Open University and the University of the Third Age and has written several books.

Gordon Macpherson was born in the Canary Islands in 1929 and educated in England and Canada. His medical experience includes work at St Thomas' Hospital, London, as a surgeon with the Royal Air Force and in general practice. He was deputy editor of the *British Medical Journal* from 1975 to 1990 and is a vice-president of the British Medical Association. He is an author and is editor of *Black's Medical Dictionary*.

Monty Meth was born in Bethnal Green, in London's East End, in 1926 and was a journalist and broadcaster, specializing in industrial affairs, for more than twenty years. He was Industrial Editor of the *Daily Mail* and won the News Reporter of the Year national press award. After seventeen years in senior management positions in industry, he became a self-employed public affairs consultant.

Eric Midwinter was born in 1932. He is a former director of the Centre for Policy on Ageing and was a founder member of the University of the Third Age. He is visiting Professor of Education at Exeter University and has written more than forty books on social history, sport, education, old age and British comedy.

Barrie Porter was born in Hull in 1936 and educated at Repton and Oxford University. He joined the BBC in 1958 as a television planning engineer and retired in 1992. He now enjoys electronics as a hobby and listening to pub jazz.

Peter Preston was born in 1938 and educated at Oxford University. After a spell in the provinces he joined the (then *Manchester*) *Guardian* in 1963, serving as Editor from 1975 to 1995. He has

241

written two novels, and his recreational activities include football, films and spending time with his four children and their offspring.

Claire Rayner was born in 1931. An ex-nurse, she is a journalist, novelist and broadcaster and is an acknowledged authority on child care, medical and allied subjects. She has written more than ninety books, from sex education to serious novels.

Jean Reid was born in 1931 and educated, at school and university, in Glasgow. She escaped from teaching into store advertising, then to a women's magazine in Dundee. After two years with the *Glasgow Herald*, she spent ten with the *Times Educational Supplement Scotland* before becoming a press officer with Strathclyde Regional Council, retiring the day it ceased to exist.

Lady Margaret Simey was born in 1906 and served her apprenticeship in social responsibility under Eleanor Rathbone. She was the first Liverpool University social science graduate and has lived and worked in Liverpool's Toxteth area most of her life, including more than twenty years as a local councillor, specializing in police matters. She is an honorary senior fellow of the university's sociology department. Her recent books include *Charity Rediscovered* and *The Disinherited Society* (Liverpool University Press).

Michael Simmons was born in 1935 and graduated from Manchester University before pursuing a career in "serious" journalism. His speciality, with the *Financial Times* and then the *Guardian*, was pre-1989 Communist East Europe. Thereafter he focused on social problems in Britain. He has written four books.

Ivor Smith-Cameron was born in Madras in 1929 and brought up in India before coming to Britain more than fifty years ago. He is a priest in the Church of England with special interests in the multi-faith, multi-ethnic and multi-cultural context in which he works. He is the first Asian to be appointed Chaplain to the Queen.

Mary Stott was born in 1907. A journalist, she joined the *Leicester Evening Mail* in 1924 and then worked on other newspapers before distinguishing herself - from 1957 - as Women's Editor of the *Manchester Guardian*. Through her pages many outstanding national women's organizations were founded. She was awarded an honorary MA by Leicester University in 1995 and a doctorate by De Montfort University in 1996. Her books include *Forgetting's No Excuse, Before I Go* and *Organisation Women*. She remains an active member of the Fawcett Society and other groups.

Kurt Strauss was born in Germany in 1930 and has lived in Britain for sixty years, not counting national service in Kenya and Egypt and four years in Brussels with Eurovision. He is an electrical engineer and worked for almost twenty-five years for the electricity industry before its privatization. He does a lot of voluntary work, especially for the Quakers.

Elisabeth de Stroumillo was born in Paris and spent her early years in India, Britain and the USA. Returning to Britain in 1945, she became a literary agent and worked for a spell with J.B. Priestley before joining *Queen* magazine. She subsequently spent some years in the airline business and later became a travel writer, then travel editor of the *Daily Telegraph*. She now writes a monthly gardens column for *Saga Magazine*.

Angela Willans was born in 1933 and is a freelance writer, the author of four non-fiction books and one novel. She was agony aunt for *Woman's Own* for thirty years and now does voluntary work for her MP and the community. She has two daughters and six grandchildren.

Help the Aged

By the year 2030 one-third of all the people who live in the UK will be over sixty. The fact that people are living longer is cause for celebration, but too many older people face a retirement of isolation, ill health and poverty after a lifetime's work and contribution to society. Everyone suffers if the wisdom and experience of older people is ignored rather than valued by society as a powerful resource.

As a national organization Help the Aged campaigns with and on behalf of older people, raises money to help pensioners in need and provides direct services where it has identified a gap in provision. Many charities throughout the UK help older people at a local level. Help the Aged works to bring these groups together to share information and expertise and fund their grassroots work. In this way duplication is avoided and the best use of money and resources is made.

Help the Aged was set up in 1961 to respond to the needs of poor, frail and isolated older people at home and overseas. *Getting a Life* is being published to mark the charity's fortieth anniversary year.

To find out more about Help the Aged visit its web site at www.helptheaged.org.uk or tel: 020 7278 1114 fax: 020 7239 1929 or e-mail: info@helptheaged.org.uk or write to Help the Aged, 207-221 Pentonville Road, London, N1 9UZ.

ISIS publish a wide range of books in large print, from fiction to biography. Any suggestions for books you would like to see in large print or audio are always welcome. Please send to the Editorial department at:

ISIS Publishing Ltd.
7 Centremead
Osney Mead
Oxford OX2 0ES
(01865) 250 333

A full list of titles is available free of charge from:
Ulverscroft large print books

(UK)
The Green
Bradgate Road, Anstey
Leicester LE7 7FU
Tel: (0116) 236 4325

(Australia)
P.O Box 953
Crows Nest
NSW 1585
Tel: (02) 9436 2622

(USA)
1881 Ridge Road
P.O Box 1230, West Seneca,
N.Y. 14224-1230
Tel: (716) 674 4270

(Canada)
P.O Box 80038
Burlington
Ontario L7L 6B1
Tel: (905) 637 8734

(New Zealand)
P.O Box 456
Feilding
Tel: (06) 323 6828

Details of **ISIS** complete and unabridged audio books are also available from these offices. Alternatively, contact your local library for details of their collection of **ISIS** large print and unabridged audio books.